SACRED EARTH WISDOM

"Sacred Earth Wisdom takes you on a high and holy pilgrimage to the power centers, the chakras, of Mother Earth. While religions encourage you to visit one power place, usually the birthplace of their founder, Anna Watts takes you to the most sacred places, the source and wellspring of the wisdom of all the ancient traditions. Keep this book by your bedside, or better yet, take it with you as you visit these sacred sites yourself."

ALBERTO VILLOLDO PHD, BESTSELLING AUTHOR OF ONE SPIRIT MEDICINE

"A truly breathtaking work, Anna weaves her captivating personal story against a stunning backdrop of sacred locations as she reveals a profound journey of insights. I can highly recommend this book to all the seekers, healers, pilgrims and dreamers of the world for its spiritual guidance. Anna is a gifted and dynamic spiritual teacher who has an exceptional talent for articulating her experiences in ways that are both memorable and transformational. This book is certain to give you restlessness for travel and will have you reaching for your suitcase or backpack and planning your next sojourn. This book is special and deserves pride of place on your bookshelf."

LISA FITZPATRICK, BESTSELLING AUTHOR AND SACRED WOMEN'S BUSINESS COACH

SACRED EARTH WISDOM

A Journey of the Heart & Soul to the Healing Sites

ANNA WATTS

SPIRIT WAY

Copyright © 2017 by Anna Watts

Published by Spirit Way www.spiritwayhealing.com.au

Distribution: Amazon (USA), Lightening Source (Aus)
Editing: Azriel Re'Shel
Cover image: Anna Watts
Cover design: Pixel Studio

All rights reserved. No part of this book may be reproduce by any mechanical, photographic, or electronic process or otherwise copied for public or private use – other than for "fair use" as brief quotations embodied in articles and reviews – without prior written permission of the publisher.

The author of this book does not dispense medical advice or prescribe the use of any technique as a form of treatment for physical, emotional, or medical problems without the advice of a physician, either directly or indirectly. The intent of the author is only to offer information of a general nature to help you in your quest form emotional and spiritual well-being.

National Library of Australia Cataloguing-in-Publication entry

Creator: Watts, Anna, author.

Title: Sacred earth wisdom : journey of the heart & soul to the healing sites / Anna Watts.

ISBN-10: 9780648072003
ISBN-13: 9780648072010

Subjects: Watts, Anna.
Healers--Australia--Biography.
Spiritual biography.
Spiritual healing.
Sacred space--Australia

ISBN-10: 0-6480720-2-9
ISBN-13: 978-0-6480720-2-7

*Dedicated to the Earth Guardians
and the Water Protectors of Pachamama*

Table of Contents

Introduction 1
The Earth Speaks 1
Earth Chakras & Vibrational Essences 7
    Where Are the Earth Chakras? 7
    Creating Vibrational Essences 9
Crown Chakra – Machu Picchu, Peru 13
    Seeing the Bigger Picture 13
    Synchronistic Meetings 15
    Rainforest Healing 18
    Temple of the Condor 20
    Heart Opening Healing 25
    Healing Inspiration from Machu Picchu 31
Third Eye Chakra – The Ganges River, Varanasi, India ... 35
    Twin-flame Meeting 35
    Following the Yogic Path 37
    Love Affair with Africa 38
    The Holy Waters of Varanasi 43
    Healing Inspiration from Varanasi 51
Throat Chakra – The Great Pyramid, Egypt 55
    Following the Path of the Priestess 55
    Messages from Ancient Egypt 57
    Entering the King's Chamber 58
    Past Life Love Affair 65
    Healing Inspiration from the Great Pyramid 68
Heart Chakra – Chalice Well, Glastonbury, England 71
    Sacred Union Within and Without 71
    Healing My Heart 72
    Drinking from the Chalice Well 77
    Temple of the Goddess 78
    The Cycles of Life 83
    Healing Inspiration from Glastonbury 89
Solar Plexus Chakra – Uluru, Australia 93
    Call of an Ancient Land 93
    Message from Uluru 94
    Love is in the Rock 100
    Return to the Heart of Australia 102
    Respecting the Grandmothers 109
    Protecting the Sacred Waters 110
    Healing Inspiration from Uluru 112

Sacral Chakra – Lake Titicaca, Bolivia & Peru 117
    Entering the Womb of Mother Earth 117
    The Gift of Receiving 118
    The Pilgrim's Way 121
    Islands of the Sun and Moon 123
    Amaru Muru – Stargate Doorway 128
    Shamanic Meeting 130
    Healing Inspiration from Lake Titicaca 134
Base Chakra – Mount Shasta, California, North America 137
    Nature Orgasm 139
    Rocking my Foundation 142
    Sisterhood Healing 144
    Magic Mountain 145
    Wesak Festival 151
    Healing Inspiration from Mount Shasta 154
Giving Birth and Beyond 159
Acknowledgements 163
About the Author 164
References 166

"When you travel, you experience, in a very practical way, the act of rebirth. You confront completely new situations, the day passes more slowly, and on most journeys you don't even understand the language the people speak. So you are like a child just out of the womb. You begin to be more accessible to others because they may be able to help you in different situations. And you accept any small favour from the gods with great delight, as if it were an episode you would remember for the rest of your life.

At the same time, since all things are new, you see only the beauty in them, and you feel happy to be alive. That's why a religious pilgrimage has always been one of the most objective ways of achieving insight."

The Pilgrimage, Paulo Coelho

Introduction

The Earth Speaks

As I stand gazing up at the sacred rock, the luminous full moon appears to be balancing on its edge. I feel a shiver go through my body and I know with every cell of my being that I have to live in this ancient land. I have no idea how this could happen, yet it seems completely right and true in this moment. Here in the moon shadow of the rock, the vibration of trust is so strong; I feel completely supported by the Spirits of the Land.

This pivotal moment out at Uluru, the heart of Australia and the Solar Plexus Chakra of the planet, was the beginning of a huge transformational time in my life. The change saw me leaving my family and friends to move 12,000 miles across the world from Great Britain to live in Sydney, Australia. I knew no-one there but I was compelled to listen to my calling.

During the early months of living in Sydney, I had plenty of time to focus on my spiritual growth. I spent many hours alone, exploring my new home on the edge of the harbour. I had only spent two days in this beautiful city prior to emigrating and I was keen to get to know the area. My weekends were filled with long walks through the spectacular national parks, meditating on sandstone rocks overlooking pristine beaches and beginning to connect with the land. I felt at home in my new climate, although at times was lonely, and had the subtle feeling that my life was changing beyond recognition. My move from England to Australia had clearly put me directly on the next step of my soul path – although I didn't know it at the time.

In the following year I immersed myself in self-exploration, something I did not have the time for in England. I studied spiritual healing, trained as a yoga teacher, learnt massage and gave away a highly successful career in advertising & marketing. My personal life was also transforming, and after a year apart, my fiancé joined me in Australia, we married and I became pregnant with my first child.

In my spare time I read many books about spiritual growth and picked up local magazines, which advertised new age events such as meditation groups, yoga classes and healing circles. One of these magazines was called "Southern Crossings." It was here that I first saw the map of the *Planetary Chakras* in an article titled *'Where are the Earth Chakras?'* by Robert Coon. 2

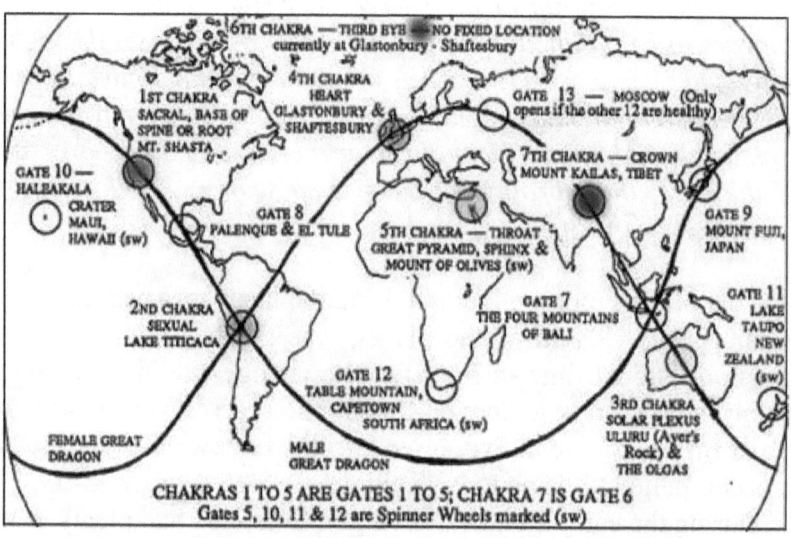

My immediate and spontaneous response to seeing this map was: *"I must visit all of these places in this lifetime!"* It was a reaction of absolute certainty and commitment. I was familiar with the human chakras, wheels of light within our energy body, but I had never heard of chakras relating to the earth. Of course, it made sense to me, if we believe our planet is a living, breathing entity, she would naturally have an energy system similar to ours. I studied the map and realised I had already been to the Heart Chakra point in Glastonbury, England and to the Solar Plexus at Uluru, Australia. If my powerful life-changing experience at Uluru was anything to go by, it was clear that these sacred sites, or chakra points, would be potent places to visit.

Little did I know that this map would be the catalyst initiating a pilgrimage that would take me all over the world to some of the most remote and spiritually significant centres on the planet. However, it took several years for me to realise the full meaning of this 'soul message' and to gain clarity about my purpose as a spiritual healer and earth keeper. There were many stages along the way that were important steps in learning to follow my inner guidance, trust my heart and discover more self-love.

Leaving the stressful business world and retraining in both childbirth education and spiritual healing was a significant move in this process. When I began to follow my heart's calling, I started to find myself in the right place at the right time. New doors opened and my role supporting women and families in their transformation to becoming parents continues to give me enormous fulfilment and joy. My work as a spiritual healer has also given me the opportunity to support many clients in times of challenge and growth. It is a privilege to work with each and every person in this role of deep trust and connection to spirit, and to see them embracing positive change in their lives.

On a personal level, it has been a profoundly transformative time on my soul path. I know without a doubt, none of this would have occurred if I had not listened to my inner guidance on that full moon night at Uluru all those years ago and put the wheels in motion to move to Australia. Looking back, I now understand the way in which my energy body or vibrational field was changed by my time at Uluru. I received what I call an 'energy upgrade'. This occurs when the energy frequency of a sacred site is higher than our own energetic vibration. Spending time there offers the chance for our auric field to be cleansed and recalibrated to match the higher vibration of the site. This will create profound change and transformation in our lives when we are ready to follow the signs.

The sacred sites around the world are steeped in the history of the ancient peoples who understood the significance of the Earth's power points. They are often located where ley lines cross in the landscape. The ley lines as they were named by the Druids, or songlines as the Aboriginal people call them, form a grid-like pattern linking one point to the next, in an intricate Global Grid. The most significant of these places can be viewed as the *Chakra System* of

Mother Earth—powerful vortexes which allow us to access the timeless wisdom contained within their energy field.

Our ancient ancestors knew that these vortexes, or gathering places of the earth's energy, were sacred, and they considered them to be multi-dimensional portals to higher consciousness. In present time, visiting the sites can be a life-changing experience—activating and energising our 'light body' thereby giving us new inspiration and clarity on our soul path, with greater awareness to consciously creating our own destiny. I believe visiting the sacred sites is a two-way exchange of energy – the natural intelligence of the site offers healing for us, and we in turn, act like an 'acupuncture needle' to bring greater awareness and alignment to the earth when we stand consciously in these places of power.

There are many important sites all over the world, near and far, each one significant in its own right. Individual places will call to different people; there is no defined place of ideal alignment on the planet for everyone. The map that I followed clearly resonated with me. It gave me the inspiration to begin my journey and to listen to my heart's wisdom. It is my wish that this book may inspire you to explore the landscapes and cultures that summon your heart and support your own spiritual journey.

Over the twenty-eight-year process of visiting the seven sites, I have trusted my intuition to guide me as to which place to visit next. It felt right to wait until a particular earth chakra began calling to me—at first in a subtle way perhaps coming to me in a meditation, and then becoming stronger. It was not a conscious or mental process of creating a travel itinerary, but more a natural organic unfolding of the path to be taken. Although I have written this book in order, from the Crown Chakra down to the Base Chakra, the individual journeys to the earth chakras happened in their own divine timing.

Visiting sacred sites and meeting with teachers around the world has greatly enhanced my understanding of the magical, the mystical, the shamanic, and the way indigenous cultures embrace healing as part of daily life. I have heartfelt gratitude for all the guides and mentors, in both the physical and spirit realms, who have played a part in my pilgrimage of healing and transformation.

There is an Irish blessing that begins with the words *"May the road rise up to meet you"*. This is how I feel when a sacred site begins to call to me; any obstacles fall away, the way becomes clear and before long, I am enthusiastically making travel plans.

Earth Chakras & Vibrational Essences

Where Are the Earth Chakras?

When I mention the earth chakras, the first question I am asked is 'Where are they?' This is often followed by a reflection on a powerful place the person has visited that must surely be an earth chakra. This is true; places such as Hawaii, Africa, Bali and many other countries all have their own power spots. Some of these are 'spinner wheels' or connecting points on the Global or Planetary Grid and every one of the sacred sites around the world is a place of significance.

When we compare Mother Earth (Gaia) to a human body, we get a clearer picture. The human chakra system is commonly referred to as having seven major chakras, coming from the Hindu or yogic tradition. There are also 114 mini-chakras and another 72,000 nadis, which can be cross-referenced with acupuncture and shiatsu points. Our own energy body is a complex network of connection points, and so it is with the earth chakras and the Global Grid. We do not have to travel far to find a place of power where we can connect with the landscape to feel aligned and energised.

On the other hand, we may occasionally feel repelled by the thought of visiting a particular place. When I first saw the earth chakra map, Mount Kailash in Tibet was indicated as the crown chakra. At the time I remember thinking this may be the only place that I would find challenging to visit. Later, I recalled an unhappy past life in Tibet, where I had felt so desperate I ended my own life by throwing myself off a high mountain peak. In that lifetime, my present-time lover had been a monk and a close friend. In the past life, he had put my soul to rest and ensured the Buddhist death rites were conducted on my behalf. My spirit finally found peace, yet I had no desire to revisit the place where I had carried so much distress in the past. I put Tibet on the back burner and continued my quest to the other chakras, always trusting the mission on my soul path would unfold in the perfect way.

Some years later, just before my trip to Peru in 2009, I read a book by well-known spiritual teacher, Drunvalo Melchizedek, called *Serpent of Light – Beyond 2012*, in which he explores the idea of the planetary crown chakra moving from Tibet to the Andes in South America. Drunvalo shares, *"This Serpent of Light and the hundreds of indigenous tribes and cultures have secretly helped guide this spiritual energy from Tibet to its new home in South America. Coming out of Tibet into India, it then moved in a snakelike manner to almost every country in the world until it reached Chile, the new home of the Earth's Kundalini, the new 'Tibet'."* [3]

When I read the book, I had the feeling this shift from Tibet, a *patriarchal* society, to South America, a *matriarchal* one, was significant for the planet at this time as we moved into a time of great healing for the sacred feminine. In South America, the honouring of the feminine is more apparent by the daily acknowledgement of the Goddess Pachamama or Earth Mother. Even in Christian terms, the worship of both the Virgin Mary and Mother Mary, as female deities, appears to be more prevalent there, too. I also understood that the year 2012 was indicated by ancient civilisations, including the Mayan calendar, to be a turning point in time when greater balance would come about on earth.

Drunvalo continues *"Not only is this a shift of spiritual power from the male to the female, but it is also a spiritual power shift from Tibet and India to Chile and Peru. The Light of the World that has been nurtured and expanded with the Tibetan and Indian cultures is now completed. Its new reign has just begun in Chile and Peru, and soon it will affect the hearts of all mankind."* [4]

My own heart was calling me to Peru. I trusted this, and made the decision to visit the temples of Machu Picchu—intuitively linking with it as the new crown centre energy of the earth. These ancient temples, dedicated to the Sun God – Inti and the medicine of the Condor, would prove to be in perfect resonance with the crown chakra connection to source and with the divine.

I later learned that many of the world's spiritual leaders, as well as indigenous teachers, acknowledge that the energy of the planet shifted during the Harmonic Convergence in 1987, from the masculine energies of Tibet to the feminine energies of Peru, and more particular, Lake Titicaca, Machu Picchu, and the Sacred Valley of the Incas.

Creating Vibrational Essences

Vibrational medicine, in the form of healing tinctures and remedies, has been practiced widely in ancient civilisations, including Egypt and Atlantis. Today, vibrational medicine includes homeopathy, Bach flower essences, gem elixirs, light essences and aromatherapy. A vibrational essence captures the healing properties of the core signature (energy pattern) of an object, being or landscape. This may be of a flower, a crystal, a symbol, sacred place, or of a particular realm, such as angelic or fairy essences.

Creating vibrational essences is a highly intuitive and transformational experience, requiring clear intention, a deep connection to spirit and trust in the process. When we create an essence, the remedy is co-created with nature and with the divine; the process is a two-way exchange and offers a blessing back to the earth. Vibrational essences offer a subtle, yet powerful way to establish balance in the chakras, the aura and the physical body to support spiritual wellbeing.

When I first began to visit the earth chakras, I had no thoughts of making essences. I was not guided to do this until the year 2000; whilst attending a flower essence workshop with Kaliana Rose, a gifted healer and founder of Rose of Raphael. I received the clairaudient message within the first ten minutes of sitting in the workshop: to begin creating essences at the sacred sites. This was a moment of such clarity and certainty that I knew immediately it was to be my new path.

I am often asked "How do I know if I am on my soul path?" My response is an invitation to explore these questions, "What do you absolutely love doing?" or "What really makes your heart sing?" The other sign of fulfilling your soul purpose is when something *finds* you, and this is the case for me with the vibrational essences. My intuitive guidance was so strong I felt compelled to follow the call.

The workshop inspired and motivated me to continue my earth chakra pilgrimage, which would now mean re-visiting some of the places, only this time to create an essence. I went on to create seven vibrational essences from the major earth chakras, a mission that took 28 years and many air miles.

These unique remedies are also referred to as 'Landscape Essences' as they capture the ancient wisdom and vibrational healing properties of a landscape or sacred site in the mother tincture. The *Sacred Planet Essences* offer the gift of aligning with the planetary healing energies of Mother Earth.

The first landscape essence created was on the beautiful island of Bali, at the Mother Temple in Besakih, high on the slopes of Mount Agung. The site is the largest and holiest temple of the Hindu religion on the island, and is built on six levels, terraced up the slope of the mountainside. The vast temple complex includes three main temples dedicated to the three Gods – Shiva the destroyer or transformer, Brahma the creator and Vishnu the preserver.

On the original map of the earth chakras, Bali was shown as a 'spinner wheel', and the centre of *purification* for the planet. It indicated that all the earth currents passing through Bali would be purified for healing. This resonated with me, and I chose to initiate the journey of the planetary essences on the exotic *Island of the Gods*.

I had visited Bali several times. I loved the warmth of the people, the beauty of their daily devotional practice and the cleansing rituals. I felt safe and at home on the island, but this trip was a different undertaking. My wish was to create the essence inside the Mother Temple, a place I knew was sacred to the local people and where visitors were not always welcome. I prayed to the Goddesses and Gods for guidance and protection as I prepared to visit the temple. I bathed and dressed appropriately in a long sarong, covered my arms and decorated my hair with sweet-smelling frangipani flowers. On the trip to the temple, I made the intention for my *path to be clear*, and although there were many guides and touts hustling for business around the ornate entrance, I managed to avoid them.

I made my way to the lower courtyard, the first platform, where it is customary to make an offering to the Gods. I received a blessing with holy water from a female priest, who smiled whilst pouring the water from the sacred mountain into my hands; I felt welcomed. I slowly began to climb the many steps through the centre of the complex of more than 80 individual temples. I hoped to make the essence alongside the highest pavilion—a platform reserved for Hindu worship and not usually open to visitors.

When I reached the top, there was a grassy bank around the temple and this is where I sat to meditate before setting up the bowl for the essence. With no-one around, I closed my eyes and began to tune into the tangible spiritual energy of the holy mountain. Before long, I felt a presence nearby and opening my eyes, I saw a priest dressed in traditional white clothing and a headdress standing in front of me. My first thought was he may ask me to move, but surprisingly this was not the case. "You are meditating," he gently affirmed, "Would you like to come inside?"

He invited me to join him in the high temple and was curious when I asked if I might place the bowl of water for the essence in front of the enormous statues of the Gods. He happily agreed and seemed open to the idea of capturing the vibration of the temple in the water to share with others. I was enormously grateful to be offered this time to experience the extraordinary power of the Mother Temple. When the essence was complete, the priest offered me his assistance to bottle it and sent me on my way.

With my mission complete, my feet literally flew down the 1,700 steps. I felt elated and joyful to have fulfilled my intention, and to have been given both access to the temple and heartfelt support to make the essence. This uplifting experience would pave the way for future trips to some of the most remote and sacred places around the world. My vision to travel to the earth chakras now felt real and within my reach.

Chapter 1

Crown Chakra – Machu Picchu, Peru

Seeing the Bigger Picture

I have a vision...

Awakening in the pre-dawn light, I am a young Inca girl. I quickly dress in my simple woven tunic, tying it around my waist, and then strap my leather sandals onto my feet. Adding the customary band around my head, I am ready for the day. With the chill of the morning air against my skin, I leave my simple abode and begin to make my way across the neat terraces cut into the mountainside. My destination is the Intihuatana Stone or 'hitching post of the sun', one of the highest points in our community, where the members of my tribe come to gather in silence as we prepare to greet the morning sun.

My friends, girls my age, are also making their way to the point where a large carved rock indicates the time of day when the sun casts a shadow on its stone. For now, we are still in the pre-dawn shadow of the mountains as our village rests on a slightly lower plateau, cradled by the surrounding mountain range.

We move quietly across courtyards and past temples where ceremonies take place at special times of the year: celebrations and rituals to mark the passing seasons, where we give thanks to Pachamama (Mother Earth) for her gifts of abundance. Many of our rituals worship the Sun God (Inti) showing our appreciation for the nourishing and life sustaining warmth of the sun as our primary source of wealth.

I begin to climb up the steps towards the Stone, quickly now to be sure I am in my place when the first rays of the sun reach our plateau. We stand together in oneness. There is no hierarchy, only our equality as men and women and the honouring of each person.

Gently at first, the light changes as the sun begins to shine over the distant peaks.

We begin to chant softly... I close my eyes to bask in the first gentle rays of light on my face as the sun emerges from the shadowy peaks. I open my crown chakra, as I have been taught, to receive the golden liquid light into my whole being. My third eye awakens, as the light flows into my body, and I feel it moving down through my throat and flooding into my heart centre. Here it becomes a golden lake encircling my chest. The light swirls into the back of my heart chakra, loosening the muscles between my shoulder blades, to allow my wings to open easily.

Reaching up with my arms, I spread my wings, as the warmth continues down through my lower chakras, my organs and veins, until every cell is bathed in liquid golden light, right down to the tips of my toes. My light body is now vibrating at 'gold' and I give thanks to the sun as this golden vibration pulses through me, overflowing and grounding down into Pachamama. I am a conduit of healing light for the Earth.

As the morning ritual comes to a conclusion, my feet carry me lightly down the steps past the Tree of Life, the only standing tree in our community, to the Condor Temple. Here I bow before the large stone altar to make an offering – again giving thanks to the sun and in acknowledgement of the powerful Condor Medicine – the gift of divine connection, higher wisdom and the conscious intention to embrace a spiritually aligned path.

Synchronistic Meetings

The first time I ever thought of Peru was back in 1985 when I was staying on a floating lodge in the Amazon in Brazil. I had miraculously won a holiday to Rio de Janeiro in a marketing competition and felt compelled to make a side trip to the lodge deep in the jungle. A local guide suggested it was possible to navigate through the rainforest from Brazil, following the banks of the Amazon all the way to Peru. When I expressed surprise at the terrain and the distance, he laughed and said, "Well, we could take a horse for you!"

After that I started to learn about Peru and gather pictures, particularly of Machu Picchu. I felt drawn to the culture and experienced a connection with 'bird tribe' energy in my meditations. I had a picture of Machu Picchu with its vivid green terraces and ancient ruins on my vision board for at least ten years before I got there. As a long-time vision board creator, I have learnt to trust in 'divine timing' that is always in alignment with our 'highest good'. The 'Universe' hears our request and delivers the results at the perfect time. In 2009, a series of synchronistic events had me journeying back to the Amazon and on to Machu Picchu.

I had heard of the Brazilian medium and healer, known as John of God, a name given to him by the local people. I understood people seeking a 'cure' for cancer or other life threatening illness would travel to his healing centre in Abadiania, a small rural village near Brasilia. There were stories of the unusual psychic surgery practices used by the 'spirit doctors' who worked through Medium Joao, as he is known in Brazil. I also knew a woman with breast cancer who had visited him and she had come to a place of wonderful trust and acceptance before her death.

In my work as a spiritual healer, I understand the soul has its own destiny and plan in the greater scheme of existence. It is not always in our highest good for our soul to continue earth-side... Several of my clients have been through the experience of serious illness and I feel my role is to support them in coming to a place of peace and acceptance, regardless of the final outcome. In fact, I have had several 'visitations' from clients who have passed over. They have all been excited to share their experience of limitless expansion in the spirit realm with me.

In 2008, my dear friend Radhika, who was just recovering from surgery for bowel cancer, met John of God. She attended his spiritual healing retreat in New Zealand, at Lower Hutt, her place of birth. On arrival at the retreat she heard the words in her head "You are not sick" and immediately knew she had fully recovered, even though she had not followed the doctor's recommendation of chemotherapy.

On returning from this healing retreat, Radhika was keen to share her experience and told me about the John of God Healing Centre in Australia (The Australian Casa). It happened to be at the top of a hill on a beautiful property, just three kilometres up the road from my home in Mullumbimby, Northern New South Wales.

I immediately started attending the powerful weekly 'current' meditations, where a direct link to Medium Joao and the healing energies of the Brazilian Casa was established for us to enjoy. The energy during these 'current' sessions was profound. I have meditated in sacred places all over the world, and this hour and a half of closed eye meditation was an experience unlike any other. The essence of pure bliss combined with a feeling of cleansing, rejuvenation and joy washed over me like a waterfall.

I had no thoughts of visiting Brazil at that time; however, each time I sat in the current meditation, I would be taken for a 'spin' over the landscapes of Brazil. I felt as if I was flying down low over the rainforest canopy, above the Amazon River, meeting brightly coloured parrots and noisy macaws hovering above the treetops. Then swooping up and soaring over the continent down to Rio and around the huge white statue of Jesus – Christ the Redeemer – standing with arms out-stretched as a guardian over the harbour. I would then travel over to the extraordinary Iguazu Falls on the southern border between Brazil and Argentina. All of these places I had visited in my earlier trip to Brazil, yet I had no conscious desire to revisit this amazing land until now.

Around the same time, another series of events rekindled my interest in Peru. My neighbours mentioned an old friend they had met up with for breakfast. He was a psychologist who had been studying with the Shamans of Peru for many years. I asked what he was doing here in Byron Bay, and they told me he was giving a talk about his Four Winds School of Energy Medicine and Shamanic

Healing and that he had invited them to join him on a trip to the Amazon in Peru.

This conversation took place on a hot summer evening in their swimming pool at around six o'clock. When I asked where and when the talk was being held, they said, "At six thirty in Bangalow", a nearby town. Within minutes I had jumped out of the pool, raced home, dressed and driven to hear the talk.

I arrived at the venue just in time for the presentation. Alberto is a charismatic speaker. He has one of those faces which could come from many cultures, in one moment looking like a young Native American, the next like an elder and South American Shaman. During the evening he talked about shamanic practices and the teachers (Inca Elders) he works with in Peru, and then guided us in a soul retrieval meditation to reconnect with any parts of ourselves which may have been left behind in other lifetimes.

The wealth of wisdom he shared included the concept, held by ancient civilisations, that time is not linear as indicated by Western calendars, but time is circular and turns like a 'wheel' or a figure of 8. The future can reach back in time and pull you forwards into the future. In sacred time (circular time) the operating principle is synchronicity. Alberto continued to share, "When you live in linear time, you get Western medicine. In circular time you get sacred medicine. When you are in 'right relationship' with time, the train leaves when you get there!"

At the end of the evening, I joined the long line of people waiting for books to be signed; I wished to thank Alberto for his insightful talk. When I mentioned our mutual friends who may join his group in Peru, he looked me straight in the eyes and said, "Why don't you come too?" I knew that nearly all of the participants on the trip were students with Four Winds and felt privileged to be invited to join them.

Immediately following this meeting, time appeared to be speeding up and everything started to fall into place – synchronicity was coming into play. A couple of days later I was invited to watch a movie about the coming planetary changes in 2012. Unbeknown to me, the documentary featured Alberto Villoldo sitting in ceremony with the Inca Elders. As I took in the magical scenery of the Andes and the Sacred Valley, I made my decision to join the Four Winds group in Peru.

Of course, I could not go to South America without visiting John of God in Brazil too, so travel plans were quickly made to fly to Peru and spend time in the Amazon. Then I would independently explore the Sacred Valley and, most importantly, finally visit Machu Picchu. This would be followed by a marathon trip across the continent from Cusco to Lima to Sao Paulo to Brasilia and on to Abadiania, the home of John of God.

Rainforest Healing

Our group meets in the dusty town of Puerto Maldonaldo. From there we will travel down the river by motor canoe for two hours to the lodge. The river here is wide and open, very different to my last experience of the Amazon when we stayed on the floating lodge, in a small tributary. Soon the sounds of the jungle begin to resonate all around us, rainbow-coloured parrots, macaws and chattering monkeys call out, as the boat makes its way through the calm water. Eventually we come to the Eco Lodge, on the banks of the Amazon, with a cluster of small cabins set in twenty five hectares of virgin rainforest – heaven!

Our first meeting with Alberto and his new wife, Marcela – who is initiated into a linage of female shamans herself – takes place in a large hut surrounded by jungle. Sitting in circle, we begin to share our personal stories and to set intentions for our time here. It is so precious to be here, I already feel like crying tears of release into the earth.

As I ponder my highest intention, here in this magical place, my heart is open and empty to receive love; my purpose becomes clear:

"To step into my new role in life when my youngest daughter is finished school. To live my destiny in love. To be fully who I am. To be in service to Mother Earth. To walk the beauty way supported with abundance and love."

Before coming on the trip, I was feeling confused as to how my life would unfold once my youngest daughter left home. My primary focus over the past ten years had been mothering my two daughters – a role I loved for the soulful connection we shared. My sacred birth education and spiritual healing work had always been on a part-time basis, to fit around school schedules and holidays. With Amber about to fly the nest, I had begun to question if I should now get a full-time job to support myself and the beautiful property I owned near Byron Bay. I loved my work with a passion. Supporting others in times of transformation, such as pregnancy, birth and life transitions, was enormously fulfilling. However, it was not fully supporting me financially and I wondered if working in more regular employment would be a better option. Here in the depths of the Amazon rainforest I was hoping to gain clarity about this decision.

The Four Winds Society teaches the ancient traditions of the Inca Medicine Wheel, Alberto is a Shaman having spent many years apprenticing with the traditional medicine men and women. I was already familiar with the power of native teachings and had created a ceremonial medicine wheel at home to honour the four directions, the seasons and natural cycles on my land. There are many different ways of working with the healing energies of the medicine wheel from the different tribes and nations around the world. Alberto works with the symbols of the Serpent, Jaguar, Hummingbird and Condor sitting in the four directions.

As soon as I arrived in the Amazon, I, too, began to connect with these totem animals. In one dream, I am at work and my Mother arrives to tell me she has a new job (my mum had died a few years earlier). She adds that I will be losing my job, but she will try to find me a new one. As I wake from the dream, a Jaguar appears in my third eye with the message: *"Be still to hear the heartbeat of the Mother. Take in your surroundings before acting."*

The next days are spent basking in the natural healing properties of the rainforest. The air is moist against my skin as we walk amongst the enormous tree guardians, leaning against trunks that are hundreds of years old and feeling their roots connecting so deeply into the earth. Tears flow as I feel the support of these ancient ones. Chino, a local shaman, watches over me, waiting quietly beside me. He points to an enormous butterfly, which has the symbol of an eye on its wings, as it comes to rest nearby. Its message is: *"Be soft in your heart and allow the gentleness to heal you."*

Later that day I receive a shamanic healing session from Chino. I ask where he learned his skills. "From meteorite," he replies. I do not question further as my Spanish is too basic. During the session he places a large rock in each of my palms. I lie with eyes closed as he conducts a cleansing ritual and heart healing ceremony. When I open my eyes I see the rocks in my hands are pieces of meteorite, it feels as if stardust is pouring up my arms and into my heart, a deep sense of relaxation and balance floods over me.

On our walks through the jungle, we encounter a huge variety of wildlife. A spider monkey suddenly jumps onto the top of one woman's head. She manages to stand completely still until our guide throws a piece of fruit to distract it. Only when it has swung off again, does she break into squeals of laughter. We visit a lake full of caiman (tiny crocodiles) lying peacefully in the water. When swimming, they use little effort, moving gently through the water. As I sit quietly by the lake in meditation, the Hummingbird totem flies into my heart and gives me the simple message: *"Drink from your own sweetness."*

By the end of my time here I have come to a place of deep peace within and without – *"Love flows through me and within me. My relationships are an outer expression of the love within. When my heart is open and expansive, my true destiny synchronistically shows itself. I am abundantly supported to follow my heart."*

As we sit in the closing circle to say our good-byes and share our final insights, the words *"The job is within you"* come to me. The healing work I already do *is* my sacred work and I am clearly on my soul path.

Temple of the Condor

After the deeply nurturing time in the Amazon, I feel ready to begin the next part of the adventure to the Sacred Valley. This area is seen by the Incas as a reflection of the Milky Way or 'heaven on earth', with the ancient site of Machu Picchu sitting on a high saddle surrounded on three sides by the Urubamba River.

We fly back to Cusco where I instantly feel an overwhelming sensation of joy. I feel peaceful, content and inexplicably happy as we wander the streets of this mountain city.

The same day we travel by car to the small town of Ollantaytambo, which dates back to the time of the Incan Empire with its cobblestone streets and quaint plaza. There are many ancient ruins around the town including Temple Hill, the Wall of the Six Monoliths and an uncompleted Sun Temple being built in the shape of a llama. Today it is one of the starting points for the four-day hike known as the Inca Trail. It is also where the train to Machu Picchu begins its journey up the mountains each day.

We have pre-booked accommodation in a family-run hostel owned by an English woman and her Peruvian husband. She says he will meet us in the Plaza to carry our bags, as the small cobblestone streets are not wide enough for cars. We wait patiently and just when we are about to give up, a car pulls up and out jumps a Peruvian man full of excitement who, in broken English, tells us he has come straight from the hospital where his wife has just given birth to their second child!

In the following days, my natural mothering and birthing skills come into play. On her return from hospital, the new mother is trying to run the hostel, make sure the guests are comfortable, supervise her husband and look after her three-year-old at the same time as she is trying to bond and establish breastfeeding with her tiny new baby. I offer gentle healing energy, soothing words, listen to her birth experience and reassure her all is well with the baby and her milk supply. Soon afterwards her parents arrive from England to give her the much-needed practical support.

On the second day, I begin to feel the effects of altitude sickness. I am very tired and short of breath, but luckily not feeling any nausea. I know it will take a few days to acclimatise, so I drink the local remedy of coca tea (which tastes nothing like chocolate; more like green tea with sugar) and continue to take the CoQ10 tablets, which support the body's ability to use oxygen. Rest is, of course, the best remedy.

We take it easy for a couple of days, exploring Ollantaytambo, the surrounding landscape and its fascinating ruins, without too much strenuous climbing. I already love this place – the stark mountains silhouetted against the crisp blue skies, the warmth of the local people, especially the women who dress like an embodiment of Pachamama with their wide layered skirts and brightly coloured hats. As in many indigenous cultures around the world, the women carry their babies and toddlers tied to their backs with a colourful woven shawl; this is attachment parenting at its best.

Being a major tourist attraction, the tickets for Machu Picchu and the train up the mountain are not cheap. There are several different classes of train and we opt to travel up on the 'Vistadome' to enjoy the spectacular mountain views through the glass roof of the train. We will make the return trip in the less expensive economy carriage.

Many tour companies offer packages, including guides, lunch and accommodation. I have learnt from my travels all over the world, to do my research first then to visit the sacred site alone or with a friend. I avoid groups with guides who are focused on the proven historical facts, as my reason for being there is to work with my intuition and psychic awareness, to 'feel' the energy and allow the site to 'inform' me of its healing gifts.

It often amazes me when I am sitting quietly meditating at a sacred site, the amount of people being herded around by guides, quickly moving from one point to the next with no time to really settle and take in the experience. Machu Picchu was no different, in fact it was one of the only times where I was sitting against a rock with my eyes closed in deep meditation, when a tourist came up to me and asked me to move so she could take a picture!

The train journey takes about an hour and a half from Ollantaytambo, making its way up the mountains through stunning landscapes. There is a sense of anticipation in the air, as the travellers gaze out of the glass roof up to the peaks above outlined against the clear blue sky. We plan to stay overnight in Aguas Caliente the small town just below Machu Picchu. There is only one hotel at the site itself (an expensive five-star), most visitors stay in Aguas Caliente so they can easily catch the bus at five thirty in the morning to watch the sunrise.

We disembark next to the colourful markets, grab a snack and head straight for the bus to Machu Picchu. Wow! This is one of the most terrifying bus trips I have ever experienced. I am sure the driver knows what he is doing but the way the road curls around the mountain with almost vertical drops plunging over the edge to the valley below has me holding my breath. I am very happy to arrive at the gates safely.

As we enter the site there is a small path off to the left. We climb the steps and find ourselves at the peak, where most of the classic pictures of Machu Picchu are taken. The view takes my breath away, seeing the emerald green terraces and ancient ruins spread out before me, with the peak of Wayna Picchu as its guardian in the background. I have waited so long to be back here in this place which I feel is in my cellular memory from long ago, perhaps lifetimes and I am overwhelmed with gratitude.

The first day, along with hundreds of other tourists, I begin to explore the layout of this historic community. Entering through the stone gateway of the walled city, I can feel the memories stored within these enormous stones, which have been placed here so long ago by the Incas. I am in awe of the structure and layout of this place, with its neat terraces perfectly aligned along the mountainside. I wonder how on earth human beings managed to create such elaborate structures with no building equipment as we know it today.

Walking along the pathways and through the temples, I begin to remember... I recall living in harmony with these surroundings, worshipping the sun every day in ritual to give thanks for its life-giving and sustaining energy. I feel at home here and seek the perfect place to make the vibrational essence the next morning, when I will return at sunrise to capture the first rays of the sun in the pure water of the essence.

The Intihuatana Stone, sometimes referred to as a sundial, is an enormous rock with a carved pointed stone on top, the highest point in the ruins. Depending on the time of day and time of year, the stone casts a changing shadow on the rock, which indicates the different seasons. I feel sure the Inca people used this to observe the timing of their rituals. This place is one of the first points to be touched by the rays of the morning sun as it emerges from the surrounding mountains.

I pass through the Temple of the Three Windows with their amazing view across the mountainous landscape. This Temple is also called the Windows of the Universe and is said to represent each part of the world: the underground (Uka-Pacha), the heaven (Hana-Pacha) and the present or the actual time (Kay-Pacha).

Imagining the powerful ceremonies that would have taken place here in these courtyards, I climb down the steps and across the main plaza. I pass by the Tree of Life, the only standing tree in the complex, say 'hello' to the nearby grazing llamas, on my way to explore the Temple of the Condor with its huge stone altar. There is an open window in the wall of the Temple, this looks promising for placing the essence in the morning sun the next day.

Finding a quiet corner, away from the crowds, I sit down to meditate in the sun. Two tiny birds come to join me, flying in and out of my space and settling in between the stones of the wall. I am taken with their size and exquisite beauty, compared to the size of the condor in whose temple I am sitting. The Condor is the largest flying bird in the Western Hemisphere, its wingspan ranges from 274 to 310 centimetres, and they can live for 50 years or more and mate for life.

In the evening, we take the bus back to town and check into our hotel next to the Urubamba River. After a simple dinner at a local restaurant, I say good-bye to my friends and fall asleep to the sound of the water flowing over the rocks below.

Whenever the time is right to create a vibrational essence I feel my spirit is vibrationally aligning with my soul purpose. Excitedly, I pack my bag with my essence-making tools – clear glass bowl, pyramid shaped cover, pure water and the crystals I have chosen to sit beside the bowl and hold the space, helping to anchor the energy for the essence.

The next day I am awake before dawn to catch the first bus up to Machu Picchu. There are many tourists making the same trip, and as always, I trust my guidance to find the perfect place for the essence, regardless of how many people are around. We arrive at the gate and I have planned to go straight to the Temple of the Condor to set up the essence bowl.

However, once entering the site, I find my feet 'walking me' in the pre-dawn light up towards the Intihuatana Stone. I follow this impulse and climb the steps to where many people have gathered to await the first rays of the sun. Usually I would avoid large numbers of people when doing my sacred work, but this time I realise everyone is here for the same reason and all are quietly waiting to greet the sun. There is a feeling of oneness.

The energy is beautiful, some people have cameras set up, and others are gently stretching or already meditating. It feels as if we have a common devotional practice and all are grateful to partake in this ritual. I see the Condor Temple below and realise I will go there shortly, but first I will receive this sunrise blessing from the Sun God.

The sky is growing lighter as the sun makes it way upwards, still hidden behind the surrounding mountains. I stand quietly breathing and grounding myself to connect here fully, allowing my roots to reach down into the centre of the earth, the crystal core of the planet. I call on the four directions to balance and support me in my work, breathing easily and opening to receive.

The first rays of sunlight burst over the opposite peak. I feel the warmth against my face and open my eyes to see rainbow prisms of light. The golden light of the sun pours in through the top of my crown chakra, like energising liquid flowing into my third eye chakra, my throat chakra, my heart and down through my physical body.

The light raises my vibration as it continues to pour through my whole being and then flows down into Mother Earth. I feel alive, energised and ready to continue my work. Without thinking, my feet carry me down the steps and into the Temple of the Condor, where I set up the essence to capture the sun's rays as soon as they reach the window overlooking the Tree of Life.

There is no one around as I set up the essence bowl and the water, then settle myself next to it in quiet meditation. I call upon Pachamama, the ancient spirit guides of Machu Picchu and the Medicine of the Condor to bless the water with the healing vibrations of this sacred place and the rejuvenating properties of the morning sun.

In meditation, I connect with the energy of the Condor, feeling the power of its wings and the clarity of vision to see the overview—the bigger picture. The message comes, *"This essence will help you to rise above the everyday and connect with higher wisdom. You will recognise your place in the world and how you can benefit humanity. Ask yourself, 'What is your unique gift to the world?'"*

I ask myself this question and immediately feel, *"I am an Inca Priestess. I worship the sun, the moon and Pachamama. I am a radiant being and an Earth Healer."* I embody this wisdom, the deep knowing that I am on purpose with my soul path, and I give thanks.

Heart Opening Healing

The days following the magical visit to Machu Picchu are both joyful and frustrating, as I had also hoped to visit Lake Titicaca (Sacral Chakra) while I was here in Peru. The news comes; there are crowds of demonstrators protesting against mining in the Amazon on the road to Puno on the banks of the lake. Puno is the Government centre of Peru and this is where the demonstrators are trying to attract media attention. However, the protestors have become violent, throwing rocks at cars and buses, so the taxi driver we have lined up refuses to drive us there.

We check out all the options, including flying from Lima to Puno, only to find the access from the airport is along this same road. For me, time is running out as I have my international flight connection to Brazil and John of God. Eventually, I accept the lack of flow and make the intention to return another time to make the essence at Lake Titicaca.

The journey to the John of God Casa is long, including a seven-hour overnight flight from Lima to Sao Paulo in Brazil, then on to Brasilia. There I am met by one of the taxis from Abadiania for the hour-and-a-half drive to my pousada, Luz Davina, the comfortable guest house where I will stay for the next two weeks.

John of God, or Medium Joao, as he is known here, holds the Healing Current sessions here each week from Wednesday to Friday. There is no charge to attend the Casa or to receive healing; there are optional herbs and blessed water that can be purchased. At first I think Joao works a three-day week, but later learn on the other days he travels to different towns and villages to perform outreach clinics for the local people. He also runs many charitable projects in the town of Abadiania, including a soup kitchen and an orphanage.

The next morning I am up early to dress, head to toe, in my white clothing (including underwear), which is requested by the Casa. This apparently makes it easier for the spirit doctors to see what treatment is needed for each person. I feel quite devotional dressing in white, then joining the stream of pilgrims walking up the dusty road to the Casa at seven o'clock.

As soon as I walk into the Casa de Dom Inacio (Home of Saint Ignatius), my emotions rise—the energy feels exquisitely loving and my tears begin to flow. There are many people, including Portuguese guides explaining the way the Casa is run. We are told to prepare questions to take to Medium Joao when we will pass by him, after waiting in line for his blessing. The advice is to ask for what is really in our hearts and to be specific on the areas we would like to receive guidance. The guides then translate our questions into Portuguese to be given to the 'Entity'—the term used for Joao when he is embodying one of the spirit doctors.

Medium Joao arrives to a warm welcome and immediately steps onto the stage and conducts a physical 'surgery' on a young man. From where I am standing, he appears to push a small pair of scissors up his nose very quickly then the man, who seems a little dazed, is taken to recovery. I have heard how this kind of psychic surgery happens here, however, witnessing it is much less concerning than hearing about it. I later discover the Casa recommends visitors undertake non-physical surgery if they wish to receive a spiritual healing. It is only those who ask for the physical demonstration who will receive this type of intervention.

It is an auspicious day—Joao's birthday—so everyone sings Feliz Aniversário (Happy Birthday in Portuguese) and he gives a moving speech about how blessed he is to be doing this work. He then leaves the stage to prepare to receive the growing lines of people into the current rooms. People have come from all over the world and all around Brazil; some have travelled overnight and arrived in huge buses now parked outside. There are about five thousand people here to celebrate Joao's birthday.

I take my place in the line to pass through the current rooms. The energy is exquisitely beautiful and I am again overwhelmed with emotion. I allow my tears as the line moves quickly forward and before I know it, I am facing Medium Joao. He looks directly at me and simply says, "Operation – two o'clock"! I am guided away and find a place to sit in the gardens as the healing current flows through me and the process of release begins.

I am a little confused as to the answers to all my 'important' questions, but try to trust that all will become clear. By lunchtime I am exhausted, and find a hammock to lie in at the pousada for a while to wait with nervous anticipation for my spiritual intervention. There are eleven people staying at the pousada and nine of us are to receive interventions on the same afternoon. This means the owner, Catherine, will help care for us in our 'recovery' time for the next twenty-four hours, when we are expected to take complete rest, away from others, and only eat food delivered to our room. The recovery time is treated as if we have received a surgical operation in a hospital. We will come back to the pousada by taxi, as walking after an operation is discouraged, even if staying just a few metres from the Casa.

Many people make the journey to John of God because they have physical or mental illness. Others come for the spiritual benefits of experiencing the healing current—this is the case for me. So I really have no idea what type of 'surgery' I will receive during the operation. The spiritual operations take place in a clinic next to Medium Joao's current room, where the spirit doctors will work on a group of us all at the same time.

We enter quietly and sit in silence meditating. I can physically feel the presence of the entities in the room. Suddenly, it feels as if a pair of hands has entered my chest cavity and is gently opening my heart centre. I have experienced my heart chakra opening before, but this is a very different and more physical sensation, my chest feels wide open and full of light. We are sitting for around twenty minutes, during which I feel sensations in other parts of my body, such as my ear that has a perforated eardrum, and then I am told the surgery is complete.

We are guided outside, given instructions for the post-operation protocol, buy healing herbs (passiflora) to assist our recovery, and catch a taxi home to rest. We must drink lots of blessed water, rest and follow a special diet.

Back in my room, I sleep until dinner, which is quietly delivered to my room. Then again sleep through until morning. Each time I get up to use the bathroom I am guided back to bed to rest more, where I can feel the entities still doing their work. At two-thirty the next afternoon, they tell me they are finished for now, and I get up to shower and sit outside in the lovely garden. I feel totally peaceful and everything looks beautiful, sparkling in the sunlight, as if I am seeing through new eyes.

The rest of my time at the Casa is spent sitting in meditation to hold the healing current. This helps to anchor the energy for the spiritual operations that are taking place. The current session goes for as long as it takes for Medium Joao to see every person in line. On one day this is from one to five o'clock in the afternoon, a four-hour meditation! Amazingly, I find it easy to sit for this period of time, even in the uncomfortable church-like seats with Brazilian spiritual music playing in the background. The current is so powerful I find myself entering a deep place of healing very quickly.

I also enjoy sessions on the crystal light beds, a therapy which connects with the energy of the healing current through the purest clear quartz crystals, which are lined up over the major chakras. It is a very relaxing, meditative treatment; some people experience a spiritual awakening whilst lying on the healing beds. My first experience with the light bed is a sensation of floating, surrounded by dolphins that are singing and sending healing waves through my aura.

Many of my experiences during current sessions include vivid imagery and meetings with angels and religious archetypes. They are profoundly healing. On one occasion, Mother Mary appears before me sending love and healing. She shows me her pregnant belly and invites me to listen to the heartbeat of the baby with my ear. This is again a sign for me to listen to the heartbeat of Mother Earth. She then spontaneously gives birth to the baby and hands him to me to hold. After a while she draws me close to her breast and strokes my hair, as a mother would comfort a child. I feel completely nurtured by her loving touch.

When the music changes, Jesus appears and asks me to dance. Our spirits 'waltz' around the room together; I cannot help smiling at the absurdity of this experience! Not having a religious background, this is an unusual situation for me, although I have connected with powerful Christ Consciousness healing energy in the past. Jesus then tells me he wants to dance with me at the sacred waterfall in the nearby rainforest.

The next day when I visit the waterfall, sure enough, Jesus is waiting for me. First I stand under the crystal-clear flowing water, enjoying the cleansing effect of the negative ions. When I step out, my clairvoyant vision is enhanced, allowing me to see the true magic of this place filled with forest devas and fairies. I close my eyes and feel myself dancing with Jesus again in this beautiful nature sanctuary.

As my time at the Casa comes to an end, I plan to attend my last healing current session. This will be a time to express my gratitude and give thanks for all I have received here. I begin to meditate and almost immediately a voice says, "Ask for permission to own a crystal light bed." I feel confused by this message. The crystal beds are very expensive to buy and, as it is the end of my trip, I have run out of money. I also know that it is a privilege and honour to be granted permission by Medium Joao to own and offer this therapy, so I feel nervous to even ask for this approval.

Of course, all my doubts are unfounded. As soon as I stand in front of Joao the permission is given immediately for me to purchase the crystal light bed. One of the Casa guides sets up a payment arrangement with me and shows me how to pack the frame of the bed and carry the valuable crystals in my hand luggage. So the next morning I am heading for the airport, way over my baggage allowance and with no funds to pay for the extra kilos. In the taxi on the way I have the realisation – oh well it's a 'light' bed so it doesn't weigh very much! The check-in clerk is friendly and is far more concerned with ensuring all my bags are directed correctly to my destination in Brisbane, Australia, and she pays no attention to the excess weight.

    I find myself back home with a new therapy to offer my clients. The crystal light healing bed is a powerful modality in its own right and is also a perfect complement to my spiritual healing sessions. The crystal bed sessions begin to attract a new range of clients and my own abilities in healing work are greatly enhanced, too. I am reminded of my message in the Amazon, *"The job is within you"*, and I now know this is true.

Healing Inspiration from Machu Picchu – Crown Chakra

❖ ### *Honouring the Sun, the Gift of Abundance*
   As human beings we are energised by the life-giving radiance of the sun; the crown chakra (Sahasara) resonates with the golden energy of sunlight. Take the time each day to stand in the sun for a few minutes. If it is cloudy or raining, you can do the practice inside as a visualisation.

   Imagine you are a tree with roots anchored deeply into the earth and branches reaching to the sky. With eyes closed, turn your face to the sun and visualise the golden light flowing from the tips of your branches, through the crown of your head and pouring down through your body. The liquid gold flows into your chakras, cleansing, healing and rejuvenating, then continues moving down your roots and back into Mother Earth. Take a few deep breaths and feel yourself as a conduit between heaven and earth. When you are ready to complete, bring your hands into a prayer position above your head, now gently lower them to your heart-centre and silently express your gratitude for the gifts of abundance in your life.

❖ ### *Sacred Ceremony for Planetary Healing*
   In the shamanic traditions, sacred ceremonies are conducted for both personal and planetary healing. The people gather at significant times of the seasons, or moon cycles, to acknowledge, offer healing and celebrate the gifts of Mother Earth. These ceremonies will often continue for several days and nights around the equinox or solstice times—with song and dance to express gratitude to Pachamama (Mother Earth).

   Create a simple ritual for yourself: gather small objects from nature to represent how you are feeling today, perhaps a rock, a feather or a flower, then make an altar on the earth or in your home. Spend time meditating to give thanks and offer healing to our beautiful planet earth. Trust in the power of your pure intention to create positive change. You can create a new altar with the seasons or to invite a particular energy into your life.

❖ Seeing the Bigger Picture

Our soul knows the expansiveness of our destiny and guides us to the next step on our path. Yet, in times of transition, it can be hard to untangle ourselves from the day-to-day reality of a situation without getting stuck on the details. The shamanic teachings remind us there is no past or future, only present time in which we can draw on cellular memory to access our own healing. Reflecting on your life as a journey of growth for the soul is a powerful way to accept the illusion of time.

When a woman gives birth, there is a time during labour called *transition* when she may feel unable to go on. The intensity of the birthing process can bring up all kinds of fears and emotions. Supporting the mother to let go and draw on her trust in the divine can help to move through this phase, perhaps changing positions, to bring her baby earth-side. Life is a series of transitions – conceiving, growing, birthing – our ideas and ourselves.

In times of life transition, a powerful practice is to do a shamanic journey to the beat of a drum, or a guided meditation to become the condor or eagle.

Visualise yourself as the magnificent condor preparing to take flight. Relax your shoulders as you spread your wings and allow yourself to lift easily into the air. Spiral upwards until you can look down on Mother Earth below. Take in all of her beauty – the oceans, rivers, forests, beaches and mountains – feeling weightless as you soar high above the earth.

From this higher perspective, undertake a review of your life. Imagine you are floating above your life path, as you remember the events since birth and become aware of the places, people and moments in your life that have been significant. Notice events where you may have invested time or energy, and gather up any parts of your spirit which may have been left behind, simultaneously letting go of anyone else's energy that you no longer need. Try not to dwell too long on particular events; this is a simple life review, which you can then bless and release to the universe.

When you reach the present day, allow your intuition to guide you to the next step on your soul path. Ask for a vision to support this – you may see a particular place on the earth or feel yourself participating in an activity. If you wish, you can spiral down closer to take in more detail and ask for further guidance. Messages from spirit may come as symbols, feelings, objects or colours. Trust you will gain clarity later if the message does not immediately make sense to you. When you are ready, gently come back to earth in present time and write or draw your experience in your journal, trusting your higher guidance.

Machu Picchu, Peru – Historical Facts

The ancient Incan city of Machu Picchu in the Andes is probably one of the best-preserved sacred sites in the world, with its 600 terraces, more than 170 buildings and several temples. It dates back to the 15th century but was not discovered until 1911 by American archaeologist Hiram Bingham. Set on a high plateau, surrounded by the stunning Andean mountains, visiting Machu Picchu and the Temple of the Condor is a breath-taking experience.

Chapter 2

Third Eye Chakra

The Ganges River, Varanasi, India (via Africa)

Twin-flame Meeting

In a healing session:
I am sitting in an exquisite garden, surrounded by an ornate wall; the sweet scent of the flowers is intoxicating, as I watch the peacock strutting over the grass with its colourful tail in full display. The sound of bird song fills the air. Beyond the garden, the waters of the lake glisten in the sunlight. Completely content and blissful in this beautiful place, I relax back in the cushioned chair and gaze up into the tree above.

A rich red pomegranate hangs from the branches. Reaching up I carefully pluck the ripe fruit. Breaking open the skin with my hands, the red juice runs through my fingers as I bring it to my lips, tasting its sweetness. I recall the legend that each pomegranate contains one seed that has come down from paradise. I know the fruit is shared by the bride and groom at their wedding as a symbol of fertility.

My beloved will soon join me in the garden. I close my eyes and feel the flutters of anticipation in my heart as I wait. When he arrives at the gate, our eyes meet with a loving gaze as he comes towards me in this paradise, surrounded by beauty and abundance...

In the pre-dawn light I stand still like a statue as my elaborate wedding sari is wrapped and tucked perfectly around me. The weight of the jewel-encrusted fabric makes it difficult for me to walk; I must take tiny steps in my ornate wedding shoes. My hands, arms and feet are painted with mehndi (henna) in a pattern of delicate flowers and marriage symbols; gold bracelets adorn my wrists and a golden chain reaches from my ear to the ring in my nose. I cast my eyes downwards, as is the custom for the bride.

We reach the temple where the sound of the pundits chanting comes from within; I will wait inside for the groom to arrive to the sound of drumming and joyful dancing. I feel nervous anticipation moving through my body. I focus on the love we have together, which will soon be fully expressed between us. During the ceremony, we adorn each other with marigold garlands and circle seven times around the holy fire as a symbol of our marriage commitment. I have complete faith and trust our union will be divinely blessed.

Later I feel myself hovering above the sacred River Ganges (Ma Ganga). With curiosity, I follow a plume of smoke from above a funeral pyre. Coming closer, I see my own body floating on the water – I have died and my physical form is being cremated here in Varanasi, the most holy of cities. My spirit then sits on the steps beside the river reviewing this particular lifetime – I recall scenes of childhood, growing as a young woman, meeting my beloved and our marriage. I remember the births of my children – two boys and two girls, who are now grown with children of their own. There is a sense of fulfilment and a life well lived – it is time to journey on.

I gaze upon the river where a radiant image of the God Shiva appears to be gliding over the water. I offer a prayer of thanks for this accomplished life. Magically I begin to manifest bright orange marigolds from my heart centre. I pluck the flowers one by one from my heart and scatter them upon the flowing river in a final blessing.

Following the Yogic Path

When I began to study yoga in Australia, I was blessed to find a school teaching classical yoga in the Sivananda linage. In the teacher-training programme we learnt a well-rounded balance of asanas (postures), pranayama (breathing), yoga nidra (deep relaxation) and kirtan (chanting). This was a complete contrast to the exercise-focused; leotard-wearing yoga classes I had attended in England. At first it seemed rather strange. We were taught by swamis dressed in deep orange robes; they had lived in the ashram in India for many years and carried the tradition of yoga from this ancient tradition.

One of the rituals we practised regularly was the sacred havan or fire ceremony. This ritual is offered for healing and transformation, both for individuals and for planetary healing. The ancient mantras (prayers) are chanted 108 times during the ceremony; they carry a powerful vibration beyond the meaning of the words and have been recited by priests and scholars for centuries. As soon as I heard them, I felt a deep connection to the mantras—as if I knew them from another lifetime—and I began to dream of India.

During the first year of yoga training, I conceived my first child; this took me on a completely new path – the path of pre-natal yoga and spiritual birthing. My teachers suggested that I run the pre-natal yoga class. In the late 80's, yoga for pregnancy was a very new specialty field. There were few teachers and no formal accreditation or two hundred hour training courses. My main qualification was being pregnant myself!

I continued to study and teach yoga for many years. My specialty was pre-natal and yoga nidra relaxation and I continued to dream of India. It was in a yoga class that I first met Liz, pregnant with her third child, and married to a beautiful Kenyan man. Liz had spent many years traveling to Africa, guiding spiritual safaris. She also facilitated meditation and healing circles and it was this difference she brought to her adventures in Kenya. The first time she asked me if I would like to join her on a safari, my answer was a clear "No, I'm going to India!"

However, the seed was planted and my husband encouraged me to join the safari. He would take the girls to England to visit family and we would meet there later. This was in 1997 and I had no idea it would spark a love affair with Africa that would see me returning to Kenya half a dozen times over the following years. The journey to Africa prepared me for future travels and for what was to come in India. Sometimes we are not ready for the healing or lessons from a particular sacred landscape and need to trust in what is naturally unfolding.

Love Affair with Africa

The landscape of Mother Africa is spread beneath me like an exquisite piece of colourful fabric with the red, green and orange patterns interwoven. Through the window of the plane, I can almost touch the snow-covered peak of Mount Kilimanjaro. I relax in my seat and one of my spirit guides, a Native American, Chief Adario, appears in my vision.

> *I stand in front of him wearing the protective feathered cloak he has previously gifted to me; he begins to lift the cloak from my shoulders, as if I am shedding a skin like a snake. At first I feel exposed, then realise there is another even lighter cloak underneath. The new feathers flutter around my shoulders; I stand tall, shimmering in all my radiance. I begin to dance, softly moving, then faster, darting around in quick easy movements. Incredibly light on my feet, I feel like a gazelle – light and springy–with my cloak flashing and fluttering behind me like an iridescent rainbow cape.*

I feel alive and energised, as if this journey will lift a weight off me and will allow me to access more of my spirit, my Light Being.

To say the landscape of the African savannah opened my heart is an understatement. My first sight of a Maasai is of a cowherd walking along with his cattle, as we are driving to the Maasai Mara National Park. He is dressed in the traditional costume of red cloth wrapped around his body, tied at the shoulder; he carries a wooden 'rungu' or club, which gives him 'Moran' or warrior status. The vast sky is the clearest blue and the golden grass ripples gently in the breeze. The cattle quietly graze as he watches over them. My heart feels an immediate connection with the simplicity and beauty of this lifestyle, spending each day out in the open caring for the cattle, a natural and holistic way of life.

We continue to drive through the Mara reserve and witness the most spectacular sunset, a single African acacia tree is silhouetted on the horizon and the clouds appear to have rainbow prisms of light behind them. There are giraffes, impalas, zebras and elephants enjoying the evening cool. I stand up in the safari vehicle and breathe in the sweet smell of the landscape. The breeze caresses my face, and tears begin to flow down my cheeks. My heart centre opens wide and I am home. Mother Africa is holding me in her arms.

The safari is rich in cultural experiences and spiritual insights. Liz guides us in in healing circles and in meditations to connect with our African totem animal (spirit guide). We meet with elders and healers in the traditional villages and I have the highlight of meeting with a Maasai midwife in her hut. With the help of a translator, we share women's wisdom and laugh together about the different birthing practices in our diverse cultures.

One of the sessions in Nairobi is a workshop with a Kenyan businessman who teaches abundance and wealth creation. A group of us have been out at the markets all morning, bargaining for trading beads and wooden gifts to bring home. As always, the dealings of actually buying something is a drawn out process of backwards and forwards bartering, chatting to the stall holders and finally acquiring the colourful necklaces at a good price. We race back to the hotel to shower and change for the afternoon session.

At this point I began to feel very strange. My body begins to vibrate or tingle in a way that I've never felt before. It is difficult to describe the sensation—like a cross between 'pins and needles' and bubbles of excitement pouring through my veins. As this intensifies, I am literally shaking all over. I now know the experience was a rush of kundalini energy rising. However, I tried to ignore it and continued to dress and go downstairs to meet our facilitator.

Kundalini is a Sanskrit, or yogic, term meaning 'coiled one'. It is the primal (Shakti) energy located at the base of the spine. Kundalini may be represented as a goddess or sleeping serpent waiting to be awakened. Kundalini awakening is said to result in deep meditation, enlightenment and bliss. This awakening can occur through practising yoga, pranayama or meditation. It can also be brought on by taking certain mind-expanding drugs, and occasionally it happens spontaneously.

The first things I notice about Grant are his startlingly blue eyes and his smile. I am preoccupied by the sensations in my body and do not initially realise this rush of energy has anything to do with him. The workshop is fun, with a focus on living your dreams, trusting your intuition and following your heart, all things I have been endeavouring to practice.

Grant has worked with some of the most well-known spiritual teachers and healers around the world, yet I feel the strong impulse to offer him a healing session. I pluck up the courage to follow my intuition and we set a time for the following day. That night I toss and turn in my sleep, feeling both nervous and excited to spend more time with this inspiring man.

The healing session with Grant is profound. The strong vibrations continue to pulse through my body as I try to stay grounded; as always I ask for the support of my spirit guides to intuitively guide me. My sessions involve reading the light body (the aura and chakras). I then share my insights and connect with universal healing energy to support the release of past-time blockages. We work on balancing masculine and feminine energies within to create more healthy relationships in life. The session is a mirror of my own healing journey so far. At the end we both feel there is more to share and agree to have dinner together.

It has been many years since I have been out alone with a man apart from my husband. I am a little nervous but not concerned, I believe my marriage is strong and have not been attracted to another man for years. It feels important to continue to share our experiences and enjoy more time together.

When Grant comes to the hotel to pick me up, the energy between us is tangible. The intense vibration in my body is now becoming familiar; we sit for hours sharing stories over dinner, continuing over a nightcap then, still not wanting to part, we talk in the car parked outside my hotel until the early hours. It feels natural to hold hands and we are both aware of the electricity in our touch. We feel like teenagers – young, alive and excited with possibilities.

The next morning the safari group leaves at dawn to Lake Naivasha, one of my favourite places in Kenya. We drive up the Ngong Hills to the lookout where the stunning Great Rift Valley is spread beneath us and the lake glimmers in the distance. The valley stretches half the length of Africa from Lebanon in the north to Mozambique in the south and is at its deepest here in Kenya.

We stay in a lovely colonial lodge for three days, enjoy the beautiful gardens and take a trip across the lake to Crescent Island where it is safe to walk around as there are no predators and the zebra, waterbuck, gazelle and giraffe graze freely. I always love traveling to new places and often feel at home in different places, but as I sit beside Lake Naivasha I know that Kenya has captured a new place deep in my heart.

As much as I love the lake, I cannot get Grant out of my mind. We return to Nairobi and the safari group comes to an end, I am bursting with nervous excitement to see him again. It is the weekend, so he suggests a trip to the coast to stay at his beach house north of Mombasa. We will fly to the coast early the next morning so he invites me to stay at his home.

Again at dinner I am amazed how easily we slip into an intimate conversation, we open our hearts to each other and share stories of spiritual growth, love, relationships and our dreams for the future. Later we lie together and make an agreement of no sexual touch or kissing. We gaze into each other's eyes as the waves of ecstatic energy pulse through my body. I feel as if I have been missing this man all my life. When I share my feelings "What is it about me you are missing in your life?" Grant asks. "Tenderness" I reply and begin to cry. He gently holds me close, I have never felt so intimately cared for in any of my relationships with men.

The next morning we fly to the coast and spend five timeless days together. We walk the white sand beach, swim, practice yoga and share spiritual insights, but mostly we lie together feeling our hearts expand as we ride the orgasmic waves of energy flowing between us. We do not break our agreement.

Five days later, when the time comes to part, we both feel enormous sadness. There are no promises to stay in touch, simply the recognition of our deep soul connection and our individual life choices. I know that meeting Grant has changed my life path forever.

In England the reunion with my husband is difficult and disjointed. Back in Australia I discover he has been having an affair for months. After several failed attempts at regaining trust and his desire for freedom from the constraints of marriage, we make the painful decision to separate. I choose to leave the city and move with my daughters to Bellingen, a beautiful rural town on the mid-north coast of New South Wales.

Looking back, I wonder if I would have had the strength to make this decision had I not met Grant. I believe we are 'twin-flames', which is the name given to two souls coming from the same spirit being. We have just one twin-flame, as opposed to the many soul mates that we meet at different stages of our life. When we meet a soul mate, we often feel an instant connection and may become close friends or enjoy an intimate relationship together. The twin-flame connection is different and can be more challenging and intense, as well as transformative. It is said the love between twin-flames is so powerful; it forces a release of all that is not love in their lives.

In my healing work I have seen the dynamic of the twin-flame connection play out with couples who have been re-united briefly and then separated again. Occasionally this separation may be through the death of one partner; more often it is through life circumstances preventing a permanent relationship. When one of the twin-flames dies, it is not unusual for there to be on-going communication and spiritual guidance from their beloved in the afterlife. The twin-flame couples who do succeed in navigating the relationship challenges can ultimately come into a deeply loving life partnership.

I have received much healing over the years about my meeting and connection with Grant; however the clearest insights are spontaneous moments in meditation when I feel his soul close and the loving support of his spirit. In one of these moments, I asked *"Why did we even meet, just to part again?"* The answer – *"To gaze into each other's eyes and to know we are each fulfilling a different part of our soul's destiny"*. This message has given me more trust in the vastness of the spirit and acceptance of our separate soul paths. I am also the first to admit on a human physical level it does not satisfy my longing!

Grant and I only meet again briefly twice; one of those occasions is my 50th birthday, when we have a chance meeting in a restaurant in Nairobi, which is a wonderful surprise and we are delighted to see each other. Again we feel our deep soul connection and again the pain of separation when we part. For me this brings another layer of grief for healing and helps me come to a place of gratitude for our meeting and the spiritual growth we are both gaining in this lifetime.

The soul is eternal; each of our lifetimes is an opportunity for soul growth. When we become attached to this physical realm as our only place of soul connection, it can limit our understanding of spiritual growth. The words of Mahatma Gandhi reflect this belief: *"Spiritual relationship is far more precious than physical. Physical relationship divorced from spiritual is body without soul."*

My love affair with Kenya still continues to this day, my heart connection with this magnificent land is eternal. On my return from a safari in 2014, I make the clear intention *"I'm ready to go to India"* and I would prefer not to travel alone. Within days I have been invited to an Indian wedding in Gujarat and make plans to travel there with my dear friend, Kelley. We will initially spend time in Goa to relax, attend the wedding and then travel through Rajasthan before visiting Varanasi, the spiritual capital of India.

The Holy Waters of Varanasi

The sacred waters of the River Ganges came to me before I went to them. During a spontaneous conversation with yoga teachers and friends, Rishis Nityabodhananda and Diwali, I mention my desire to make the vibrational essence at Varanasi and not knowing when I will be free to travel there. Magically, Diwali produces a bottle of holy water collected from the river at Varanasi, which they have carried back to Australia.

As always, I see this as the synchronistic sign of right timing to make the essence for the third eye chakra. I prepare the bowl of water, ready to create the mother tincture using just one drop of the holy water as a homeopathic signature. There is a large statue of the Hindu God, Ganesha (known as the remover of obstacles), at the entrance to my home; this is the perfect place to place the essence where it will not be disturbed. I decorate the space with colourful marigolds, light the incense and sit in meditation in order to connect the spiritual energies of Varanasi with the mother tincture here in Australia. Once the energies are aligned, the essence will be left to infuse until I receive the guidance it is complete.

Later that evening, a friend calls and I suddenly feel very emotional and announce, *"I feel like dying!"* This is very unusual for me, as I have never suffered from depression nor felt suicidal in my life. I feel very strange, and, talking with her, realise I must be experiencing the energy of Varanasi, which is the favoured spiritual place for devotees of the Hindu religion to go to die and have their bodies cremated.

Now I understand what is happening to me and decide to run a bath with essential oils and flowers to do a personal Puja (purifying ritual) for myself. The scented water soothes me and the feeling of wishing to die passes. I see with clarity the timelessness of my soul and gain new understanding of the illusion of the physical realm. I make the intention to release any past karma associated with India and to clear the way to be more consciously on my spiritual path. I quietly chant the healing mantras over and over to myself one hundred and eight times (the sacred number), before having a restful sleep.

The following day is our regular fire ceremony; we set up the altar with statues of the Indian deities, including Lord Shiva, Ganesha, Lakshmi and Hanuman, all decorated with abundant flowers and candles. I carefully carry the mother tincture and place it on the altar to receive the powerful vibration of the mantras chanted by the group. We chant to Ganesha and to Durga (the Cosmic Mother) and ask for their blessing, followed by the Mahamrityunjaya healing mantra:

ॐ tryambakaṃ yajāmahe sugandhiṃ puṣṭivardhanam

urvārukamiva bandhanān mṛtyormukṣīya mā'mṛtāt

I leave the tincture in the moonlight overnight and bottle it the next day, feeling as if all the blessings of the sacred river, Ma Ganga, have come to me right here in Mullumbimby, Australia.

When the time comes to actually visit India, I feel prepared and open to connecting with this mystical land and following my spiritual calling. I have heard it said, "Nothing prepares you for India", but my experience with the essence, plus all my travels in Africa, put my mind at rest. My friend, Kelley, on the other hand is filled with many fears, including fear of her feet touching the ground, fear of eating the food, fear of feeling overwhelmed, fear of being ripped off when shopping—the list went on! She knew the fears were irrational but they were arising from deep inside. I agreed to support her as best I could during the trip and Kelley also spent the weeks leading up to the trip releasing the fears and preparing herself for this new culture.

Our trip began with a twenty-four-hour stay in Mumbai (Bombay). We had a room overlooking the harbour and enjoyed a trip around the city, visiting elaborate temples and shrines of the Hindu, Jain and Sikh religions. However, the place where we felt moved to tears was the small home of Gandhi, which was the focal point of his political activities between 1917 and 1934. This tiny house felt like an ashram on entering, and the pictures of Gandhi, with quotes of his teachings, touched our hearts. One of my favourites being:

"Happiness is when what you think, what you say, and what you do are in harmony."

Next stop, South Goa, where we indulge in a relaxing week of nourishing Ayurvedic treatments, enjoy good food and quiet beaches. Surprisingly, Kelley soon gets the hang of bartering and is chatting with shop keepers and trying on saris like a local.

Whilst beautiful, Goa is a predominantly Christian culture, which I do not have an affinity with on a spiritual level. I am looking forward to visiting places of significance to the Hindu religion; first we will travel to Ahmedabad in Gujarat for the Indian wedding.

I could devote a whole book to the marriage of Gabriella and Gaurav, a beautiful Australian girl and a handsome Gujarati boy who met in Adelaide. For those who have attended an Indian wedding, you will know it is not uncommon for thousands of guests to attend. This was a small wedding with just eight hundred guests, including thirty Australians who have travelled here to join the celebrations.

There are many elaborate rituals over the four days, including Mehndi, the henna hand decoration for the women; Raas Garba, a festive dance party with many performances; Agni, the fire ceremony; Graha Shanti, the prayer ritual; and Mandap, where the couple adorn each other with marigold garlands and circle the sacred fire seven times, making seven promises for their life together.

Each occasion requires a new and increasingly elaborate outfit, so the week leading up to the wedding is a busy schedule of choosing colourful clothing, having fittings and buying glittering accessories.

We have lots of fun practising dance steps (quite a challenge in a sari!), having our hair and make-up done and getting fitted by the 'Aunties' in our saris as they pull the fabric tighter and tighter around the waist to make it secure. The Aussie girls make an effort to be respectful of all the cultural guidelines, such as lots of midriff can be shown, but shoulders must be completely covered at all times.

The final ceremony takes place outside under a beautifully decorated pagoda where we shower the happy couple with rose petals as a blessing for their marriage –

> *May you fully support each other, in the journey of your life!*
> *Let your lives be one, one soul residing in two bodies.*
> *May your lives be woven together, with a strong fabric of love, harmony and peace!*
> *Lead a full life of joy, with family, friends and children!*
> *May God bless you!*

The following morning, Kelley and I leave for Rajasthan and the lakeside city of Udaipur. Our journey takes us up through the mountains, traveling through villages and communities while gaining a fuller picture of rural life in India. The first view of Lake Pichola takes our breath away and we spend the day exploring the city's narrow streets filled with exotic shops and ancient bazaars. The sacred cows wearing their marigold garlands wander aimlessly along, undisturbed by all the activity. We visit the lavish City Palace and sit in the exquisite gardens with its intricate peacock mosaics; there is an air of complete serenity and peace here.

Udaipur has been called *'the most romantic spot on the subcontinent of India'* and a tranquil boat-ride on the lake at sunset confirms this belief. We watch the sun slip behind the Aravalli Mountains and take in the vision of the floating palace with its Arabic-style turrets. The twinkling lights on the shoreline draw us back to dine on the rooftop terrace of the Jagat Niwas Palace, a 17th century haveli overlooking the lake. We are completely mesmerised by the full moon rising above the Jagdish Temple. I am smitten with this magical place and make a promise to return here again soon.

We continue our journey through Rajasthan in search of all things spiritual. Our next stop is the holy lake at Pushkar, which is said to have appeared when the Hindu creator god, Brahma, dropped a lotus flower from the sky. It is a significant pilgrimage town for devout Hindus who try to visit at least once in their lifetime.

By now Kelley is gaining confidence in dealing with the Indian culture. But she surprises me further when we arrive at our accommodation in Pushkar, a tented camp on the edge of town. I suggest she goes into reception to check out the accommodation, while I arrange the payment for our driver and stay with the car in case we need to continue on for any reason. A few minutes later, she emerges with a serene Zen-like smile "Everything's fine" she says calmly. I ask if we should check the tent first, "No it's all perfect, trust me!"

She is correct; Orchard Camp is managed by a beautiful Sikh man with a gentle nature. The staff ensure all our needs are catered to, including delivering pots of tea to our tent before breakfast and turning on electric blankets to warm our comfy beds while we are enjoying a delicious dinner. This really is 'glamping' at its best!

The next morning we go to the vast Brahma Temple. I am keen to immerse myself in the spiritual energy here and wish to receive a puja (purification and blessing ritual) with a Brahmin priest by the lake. We tour the temple with a guide, who emphasises the need for any donations to be made to the official office nearby, where a receipt will be issued. We ask to receive puja together, but are told we must each have a separate priest to conduct the ritual.

As soon as the priest begins to chant the Vedic mantras, tears begin pouring down my cheeks. I am deeply moved by the sound and vibration of these ancient prayers. I feel my soul connection to this ancient spiritual practice and my heart centre opens. At some point in the ritual, the priest asks me how much donation I would like to make to ensure a smooth transition for the souls of my ancestors through the afterlife. I open my eyes and tell him the amount of rupees I will donate, he asks for more but I am clear and we continue the puja. When the blessing is complete, I feel blissful.

I look around for Kelley, but she is nowhere to be seen. I ask the guide. "She had to go to the ATM" he replies "… on a motorbike". I know immediately something is wrong, and can hardly believe she has jumped out of her comfort zone and onto the back of a bike with a stranger!

When Kelley returns, she is furious and wants to leave

immediately, I just want to know how this has happened. She tells me that she was enjoying the powerful spiritual energy of the puja until the priest asked her for a donation; he then insisted she increase the amount in order to properly honour her deceased relatives and the souls of her ancestors. Being brought up as a Christian, she remembered her father had made a generous donation at church every Sunday and wished to also respect the Hindu religion. She then felt pressured to increase her donation, when she told the priest she only had a smaller amount in her purse, he replied "No problem we will take you to the ATM".

We had to laugh at this later, remembering all her fears of traveling in India and here she is hopping onto the back of a motorbike and going to withdraw the equivalent of three hundred dollars for the priest to bless her ancestors!

Coming from my blissful puja state, I stay completely calm and suggest we return to the donation office, Kelley is still upset and sceptical that this will be of any benefit. However, as we walk back. a young man, also a Brahmin priest, stops us to see if we are ok. Kelley recounts the story; he quickly makes a phone call and ensures her that the donation will be returned, adding in typical Indian fashion *"If you are not happy in your heart, we are not happy"*.

Ah India, such a place of mystery, contradiction and negotiation. Kelley is relieved when her money is duly returned, she leaves a more appropriate donation and we head back to the safety of our camp free from spiritual con artists.

A few days later, we have an overnight stop in Agra to visit the iconic Taj Mahal, where we hope to watch the sunrise. We awaken at dawn and climb up to the viewing terrace of our hotel, only to find there is dense fog completely blocking the view. This does make for some mystical photos of the exquisite architecture when we get up closer and we enjoy a chilly walk around the gardens, before leaving at mid-day as the fog begins to lift.

In Varanasi, our hotel is overlooks the River Ganges, but again everything is shrouded in fog giving it a mystical air. We can just see the outline of the ancient city in the distance and head out to explore, wearing many layers of clothing in the chilly weather. The one thing I have dreamt of doing here is taking a boat across the river at sunrise; sadly the fog is so dense we never actually see a sunrise or a sunset during our stay.

We walk for miles along the famous Ghats, steps leading down to the river, taking in the many temples and Sadhus (holy men) along the way. There are groups of pilgrims, many dressed in orange robes, standing in the water to bathe and conduct puja before sailing down the river to make their offerings to Ma Ganga; they have travelled from all over India to make this once in a lifetime act of spiritual devotion.

Next to the river, south of the bridge, is Manikarnika Ghat, the main cremation area where we watch respectfully as bodies are carried down to the water's edge to be burned. Devout Hindus consider Varanasi the most auspicious place in India to undertake this final 'rite of passage'. The men of the family are charged with the duty of sending their loved ones off to the next life. They ensure the body is washed and wrapped in golden ceremonial cloth before the fire is lit by the Doms—members of the Untouchables caste, who have the task of carrying out the cremation. The relatives wait patiently nearby until the fire has consumed the physical remains and the body is returned to dust. The women are considered too emotional to attend the cremation and wait at home until their menfolk to return for further rituals.

Whilst confronting, the ambience in this part of town is peaceful and the open acknowledgement of the body as a temporary dwelling for the soul touches my heart. I have supported several clients through the dying process and endeavoured to make their transition from body to spirit as smooth as possible. I believe death, like birth, is another aspect of life, which is part of the natural cycle of the spirit. Natural death is to honour the wishes of the individual and their family, dying at home where appropriate and giving loved ones the opportunity to be a part of this ultimate spiritual transition.

In the evening, we attend the spectacular Aarti ceremony at Dashashwamedh Ghat, where a row of priests, students of the ancient texts the Vedas and Upanishads, perform a nightly ritual of worship to Lord Shiva, Ma Ganga, Surya (Sun), Agni (Fire) and the whole universe. The altars are decorated with abundant flowers and the heady scent of sandalwood incense fills the air while the deep sound of the conch shell vibrates loudly as the priests begin chanting the powerful mantras.

The priests circle flaming brass lamps, shaped like serpents, around themselves, accompanied by songs in praise of Ma Ganga.

At the end of the ritual hundreds of people climb silently down the steps to say a prayer and set a flotilla of tiny candle lit offerings afloat on the sacred river. The powerful energy of the Aarti continues to vibrate in our hearts as we find our way home.

On the last morning we take a boat trip. Despite the invisible sunrise, the river is calm as we glide through the water and quietly express our gratitude to the mystical city of Varanasi and the many pilgrims who have gone before us. We make an offering to Mother Ganges, casting marigold garlands into the holy waters. In this moment, the sun finally peeks through the clouds – thank you Ma Ganga, the Goddess of the most holy river in India. Namaste.

Healing Inspiration from Varanasi – Third Eye Chakra

❖ Creating a Sacred Sanctuary

The path of the spiritual follower is an individual and personal one. Sitting in stillness with your self is an on-going process of inner discovery. Learning to withdraw into the third-eye chakra (Ajna) gives us the opportunity to reflect and trust our intuition. Devotional practices with a spiritual teacher or with a meditation group can also assist this process. Sit comfortably to practice this short mindfulness meditation, for five or ten minutes, to clear your intuitive space:

Gently close your eyes and allow your gaze to soften behind closed eyelids. Invite your spirit to be fully present with you for this time. If you have been busy, gently reflect on the people and places you have had contact with and separate from these, calling your spirit home. Imagine the centre of your head is your own private meditation room. If your room is full of thoughts or worries, create an imaginary 'vacuum cleaner' to clear out the thoughts and release them into the atmosphere. If you wish to retrieve them later, you can do this easily when your meditation is complete. You may find they have magically resolved themselves.

Next make your circular room beautiful – add cushions, a comfortable chair or some flowers – you can decorate it any way you like. Feel yourself relaxing back in the centre of your head behind your softly closed eyes. This is the place of your Third Eye Chakra, the more relaxed you become in this chakra, the clearer your intuition and visionary abilities.

Enjoy this place of just 'being' where you can see clearly (clairvoyance). This is your personal inner sanctuary – the sacred space to connect with your spirit. Become a witness to any images, colours or shapes that appear – without judging or feeling attached to them, simply reflecting. You may experience a sense of peace while doing this practice. If you do drift off, gently bring your awareness back to the 'present moment'. Relax for as long as you wish; establishing a regular time to practice will have great benefits.

❖ Connecting with your Twin-Flame or Soul Family

Soul Family is not necessarily the same as your biological family. A soul mate is someone who you have chosen to journey with through time as a spirit. The relationship with members of your soul family is a deep psychic connection and understanding beyond the personality level, offering clear and direct communication (often not needing words), unconditional love and support. When we meet a soul mate, or twin-flame, there is often an instant recognition or a feeling of comfort and familiarity. Spending time with soul mates enhances our spiritual growth and our intuitive connection remains strong, even if we do not see each other for long periods of time.

You can make an intention or affirmation to reconnect with your twin flame or with more members of your soul family by holding a vision at the third-eye of an infinity flow (figure of eight) of gently pulsating light between your souls coming together in harmony.

Affirmations to assist this process:
"I welcome more members of my Soul Family into my life"
"I reconnect with my Twin Flame in the light of divine love"

❖ Holding a Vision of Peace on Earth

At this time when we are yearning for world peace, we must let go of judgements and first come to a place of peace within ourselves. When we open our hearts and minds to loving acceptance of all spiritual traditions, we nurture greater respect for all peoples and religions on this beautiful planet.

Many world religions have a common thread of spiritual beliefs and teachings that acknowledge a higher source or god/goddess presence, whether their prayer is conducted inside a church, a temple or outside in nature to honour the earth. Sadly, in many countries the traditional cultural practices of indigenous people have been squashed by invasion and occupation. Sometimes we can feel overwhelmed by negative news stories and outside influences; this is the time for us to draw within.

Find a devotional practice that nourishes your soul, see yourself as a custodian or guardian of Mother Earth and hold a vision for world peace. Chanting this ancient Shanti mantra inspires peace on earth:

"Om lokah samastah sukhino bhavantu"

May all beings be happy. May all my thoughts, words and actions contribute in some way to the happiness of all beings.

Varanasi, India – Historical Facts

Varanasi, previously known as Benares, has been the spiritual capital of India for several thousand years; it is the holiest of the seven sacred cities. Situated on the banks of the River Ganges, Varanasi is known as the sacred place of Shiva. A bath or *puja* in the sacred river is believed to wash away all one's sins; for Hindus death and cremation in the city will bring liberation from the cycle of reincarnation.

Chapter 3

Throat Chakra

The Great Pyramid, Egypt

Following the Path of the Priestess

In a past-life recall:

   I am walking slowly along a pathway of pure gold towards a pyramid. Crowds of people dressed in festive clothing are lining the walkway, as I enter and begin climbing up the steps inside. The sound of chanting vibrating throughout the pyramid is intense, the words, "Isis you are the Sun" are repeated over and over.

   The time is 4.30am, close to sunrise. There is a window in the pyramid through which the sun's rays will shine on this particular day, as they do once a year. I have been carefully prepared for this important festival as a representation of the Goddess Isis. I am wearing white, an exquisite cloth spun with gold, draped over my body and held in place with a gold belt. Underneath I wear a modesty skirt of gold-dipped papyrus material. My necklace is a golden serpent, twined together at the throat, reaching down to my solar plexus. I wear ornately decorated wings, beautiful anklets and bracelets—all gold. My skin is polished with golden powder – a symbol of the sun. My head is weighed down by my headdress, a heavy golden orb representing the disc of the sun, cradled by cow horns, symbol of the Goddess Hathor.

   Once in position at daybreak, I must stand tall, supported by two guardians, spreading my elaborate wings as my headdress catches the first red rays of the morning sun. The rays will radiate from the golden orb onto mirrors placed around the pyramid so each person present will receive the light. This will be a reconnection to the universal flow of abundance and to their own inner light.

My breathing is heavy as I wait for the first rays of the sun. It is a great honour to be chosen to represent Isis. I must stay grounded in my body for the entire ceremony. It is 4.37am on this day, the only day of the year when the sun's rays will shine through this window in the pyramid.

As the light hits the golden orb on my headdress, it resembles a spinning fireball. The sun radiates directly into everyone's chakras, aligning them with golden light. The chanting becomes louder; everyone is high on the energy, merging with the first rays of the sun.

When the ceremony is complete, I lie down to rest with another orb of lapis lazuli crystal at my feet. The blue stone brings a soothing balance to the high energy I have held on my head, I can now relax, my task is complete.

In another Egyptian lifetime, I have a simpler lifestyle. This time I work in solitude, dedicated to my soul calling as an initiate in the priestess tradition of the Goddess Isis. I live close to the River Nile, conducting simple rituals to honour the seasons and the cycles of nature, celebrating the phases of the moon and blessing the land. I give thanks for the annual inundation of crops, which give sustenance to my community—a welcome sign of fertility from the God Hapi.

This is a content and peaceful life. I see myself serenely walking to the temple, along the riverbank where the blue lotus grows. I make my offering of nourishing foods, perfumed ointment and flower decorations to the Gods and Goddesses before entering the inner sanctuary. Inside I create a spiral pattern on the earth with stone tablets carved with the sacred symbols. My task is to align with the vibration of these ancient symbols, including the Ankh, the Scarab and the Eye of Horus, and offer their healing vibration into the earth for balance and harmony. I call on the Goddess Isis for her loving guidance and support as I drop into a meditative state, becoming a conduit between heaven and earth, dedicating my devotional practice to Mother Earth and the higher order of creation for now and eternity.

Messages from Ancient Egypt

The first time I had an experience of channelling; it felt like a huge pressure on top of my head above my crown chakra—as if I was wearing a really heavy headdress or a crown. This feeling came out of the blue, beginning after a brief relationship with a man that ended abruptly. Paul was strongly attracted to me from the moment we met, however I did not feel the same about him and was unsure about continuing the encounter, but I was surprised when he suddenly called it off. I was left with the strange feeling on my head and felt completely off centre. I now realise we had a strong past-life connection and through our meeting, an aspect of my soul was re-activated to remember ancient wisdom.

With the enormous pressure on my head, I went to visit Mary, my friend and co-owner of The Rose Centre in Bellingen. At this time we had been running the healing centre for a couple of years, both offering individual workshops, healing and counselling sessions. We were yet to collaborate on any projects together. Mary welcomed me and I immediately had to lie down and close my eyes. The pressure was intense and I began to hear (clairaudience) words of guidance. I spoke these out loud and Mary, realising what was happening, carefully transcribed the information.

The message appeared to be coming from Ancient Egypt. This was most surprising to me, as I had no particular interest in Egyptian history although I knew one day I would visit the Great Pyramid as part of my earth chakra pilgrimage. Mary, however, had been fascinated with Egypt since childhood. She remembered gazing at a photograph of her mother on a camel at the Sphinx in 1950, the year before she was born.

The channelled instructions were clear: I must draw the symbols of Ancient Egypt one by one and begin to make vibrational essences. The first symbol would be the Ankh – the symbol of eternal life and the key to wholeness. The vibrational qualities of the symbol were to be captured in pure water over a period of seven days and seven nights, I would then receive the guidance for the next step. As soon as the channelling session was complete, the pressure on my crown chakra dissipated and I felt centred again. It seemed the divine guidance simply had to flow through. Of course, I still had a choice as to whether to follow it or not. Over time, it became much easier for me to receive messages from the spirit realm, writing them into my journal and nowadays I can channel whilst typing directly into the computer.

Through her fascination with Egypt, Mary had acquired extensive knowledge about the history of this ancient civilisation. We both believe the initial guidance came through me to avoid this influencing the channelled information. In fact, during our yearlong 'assignment' of making Egyptian Essences, we chose not to reference other material and to put complete trust in our intuitive guidance. We both resonated with the new information and discovered our joint gift for co-creating the essences with pure intention and deep connection to spirit.

After creating the third essence, the Eye of Horus, it dawned on us the ancient symbols had a relationship with the chakra system and the ability to bring powerful healing to the light body, including the aura, the chakras and the physical body. All of the guidance referred to the sacred number seven, known as the number of 'Collective Consciousness' – spiritual awakening, inner wisdom and natural healing abilities. We went on to create four ranges of seven essences – the Symbols, Goddess/Gods, Temples and the Natural World. Later we would be guided to create Pleiadian, Atlantean and Lemurian Essences, all offering ancient wisdom for present healing.

Throughout 2001, our essence-making endeavours progressed and we felt a strong impulse to make a range of the essences in Egypt. So with great excitement, we planned a trip to visit the pyramids and the temples in September. Three days before our departure, the unimaginable happened. The events of 9/11 caused chaos in world travel, yet we felt called to continue our trip and trusted we would be divinely protected on our journey to the sacred sites of Egypt.

Entering the King's Chamber

Our journey to Egypt was uneventful, apart from the overwhelming energy of fear amongst the travellers following the events at the World Trade Centres in September 2011. It was unclear what action America would take in the 'fight against terrorism', and there were enormous shock waves in the aftermath of what had taken place. The recurring footage of the airplanes crashing into the World Trade Centre was being played over and over. At the airport in Abu Dhabi, a crowd was gathered around a large screen watching the continual replay – not a very reassuring thing to do before getting on a flight!

We arrived in Cairo late in the evening and arranged a transfer to our hotel overlooking the pyramids in Giza. We had splurged on this accommodation for the first two nights of our trip in celebration of Mary's 50th birthday and it was the only arrangement we had pre-booked. As we left the airport, I had the voucher for our hotel in my hand inside a golden coloured wallet, but by the time we arrived at the reception it was gone. Fortunately, the receptionist agreed we could go to our room for the night and provide the voucher the next day.

The Mena House hotel is set in 40 acres of verdant gardens, which is surprising, given the dry, desert setting of Giza. We walked through the moonlit gardens to our room on the second floor, stepping out onto the balcony and gasped in awe at the view of the Great Pyramid lit up in the night sky. The pyramid was literally right outside our window. Being in this ancient land was truly a dream come true.

Early the next morning I sat out on the balcony in meditation:

> *The Goddess Isis is waiting to welcome me to the Great Pyramid. She guides me inside, where we walk a spiral path into the centre of the pyramid. We slide down this spiral vortex into the point of an inverted pyramid below – a mirror image of the one above the earth, forming a diamond shape. Isis shows me a golden 'hara line' (vibrating energy cord) which reaches through the lower pyramid, down into the centre of the earth and up through the upper pyramid to the heavens. She tells me part of our soul work here in Egypt is to place the sacred symbols back into the earth, bringing the pure vibration of these ancient healing codes into present time. I begin immediately, placing the Ankh symbol into the tip of the lower pyramid, along with the word 'Life' – the main quality of this symbol. The Ankh slides up the hara line into the centre of the Great Pyramid and begins to radiate golden light out into the world.*

> *Isis tells me we must work with one symbol a day for the next seven days, Mary and I can take it in turns, but we must stay here close to the pyramids for three days, we are then free to continue the work from other places in Egypt. She adds, this energy work and creating the essences here will be easy for us to do and we will have lots of fun. Our wings will be open by the third day, with our arms stretched wide and our hearts expansive. I clearly see the image of Isis before me and as she leaves, we bow to each other in prayer and recognition of our mutual devotion to the Priestess Path.*

The morning sun was already hot as we walked the short distance to the Giza Plateau, the home of the Sphinx and the three pyramids Khafra, Menkaura and the most famous of all – Khufu, the Great Pyramid. We take in this extraordinary site, at the edge of the desert, which is the oldest of the Seven Wonders of the Ancient World and the only one still standing. Security on the plateau was high and groups of police with guns were patrolling the area, as they do in all the major tourist attractions. They did not bother us and we appreciated the fewer visitors resulting from the cancellation of all trips from the USA.

We began by slowly walking around the base of the Great Pyramid as if anchoring ourselves along the perimeter. The pyramid is built of enormous stones. It is impossible to imagine how this ancient civilisation built the structure without machinery, as some of the larger stones weigh between six and ten-tons each and there are over two million stones in total. There are many theories about how the stones were quarried, transported and put into place, yet the precise details still remain a mystery and this is why we are here – to connect with the mysteries of Egypt.

We took our time exploring the plateau, resting against the warm stones to meditate and wandering around the Sphinx that sits like a protective guardian looking out over the desert. We decided to make the essence the following day and, feeling the effects of jet lag, returned to the hotel to rest.

The receptionist was beginning to get annoyed that we still had not produced the missing voucher, and with his help I contacted the agency who arranged our airport transfer to see if it was left in the taxi. The travel agent, Sahir, is very friendly and helpful but checks with the taxi driver who insists it is nowhere to be found. We tried not to stress out when the receptionist lets us know that without the voucher, we will be required to pay the accommodation bill again on departure, an expense that would blow our budget.

Mary meditates on the golden wallet and clairvoyantly sees it underneath the seat in the taxi. I call Sahir back and he eventually agrees to try the taxi driver again. We know there is an astrological event at this time, where the planet Mercury is in a retrograde position. This occurs three times a year and often brings delays or confusion with travel and communications, so we prayed when Mercury goes into direct position again, in the next couple of days, that the missing voucher problem will be resolved. In the meantime, we rested in anticipation of our day ahead in the Great Pyramid and held the vision that we would gain easy access into the King's Chamber.

In our room the next morning, we continue our commission working with the symbols. This time the Scarab symbol is placed into the hara line, with the word *'Transformation'*. Once again golden light radiates from the pyramid throughout the world. We are now ready to make the essence.

Back on the Giza Plateau, we enter the Great Pyramid through a narrow passageway and begin to climb the high steps up through the vast hallway to the King's Chamber. It is a steep climb up the dimly lit stairway; even though challenging, I keep my balance and feel as if I have climbed these steps many times before.

We have the essence-making kit with us, but still have no idea if this will be possible, given the number of people climbing with us. We reach the door to the chamber where a tall man stands guard. He stops us suddenly and asks *"You want to meditate?"* We nod our heads. *"How long?"* he adds. I manage to splutter out *"an hour,"* and he ushers us inside the chamber. There are many people here, talking loudly, looking around examining the granite walls and the stone sarcophagus, and finally they all leave. We are expecting more people to join us, but the guard keeps his word, and we are left alone in the sacred sanctuary of the King's Chamber for an hour!

We set up the essence bowl behind the sarcophagus and sit down to meditate. We call on the Ascended Masters, the spiritually enlightened beings, to support the process here with us. We see the spirits of the Goddess Isis and Mother Mary appear at opposite corners of the chamber, followed by Jesus Christ and the God Thoth, at the other corners, holding the energy of male/female balance and protecting the space for us.

As I meditate and connect with the vibration of the Pyramid, and its significance on the planet, I feel it has a far greater metaphysical role than simply a tomb for pharaohs. I am reminded of the essence we have previously made with the pyramid symbol. One of its qualities is for all beings to *"Speak the truth from the heart"*. I am intensely aware of the importance of this concept at this time when the prospect of America going to war with Iraq is highly likely. I feel very emotional, sitting in the Great Pyramid, the Throat Chakra of the world, holding the intention for clear, heartfelt communication between nations, and a resolution that is still needed today. I feel the loving support of the Ascended Masters forming a double infinity flow of light (two figure-of-eights) between the corners of the chamber, meeting in the middle for balance and harmony.

Looking over at Mary, she appears to be overwhelmed with grief, and she shares the message that has come to her *"We welcome peace and balance for the next sixty thousand years for the planet."* This concept seems impossible given the present political situation. However, we feel it is important to speak this affirmation out loud three times, as a prayer for planetary healing. The words resound through the chamber, reactivating this powerful healing portal. We then begin to sing and chant, joyfully raising our vibration, welcoming peace on earth and completing the Throat Chakra Essence.

As we leave the King's Chamber, the guard has disappeared and we have no opportunity to thank him for his role in helping us to create the essence. We make our way slowly down the steps and our legs begin to feel sore from the climb and the intense energy work—it is time to rest again.

Back at the hotel, the missing voucher has magically been delivered to reception and all is well. We book another night of accommodation to finish our sacred work here in Giza. At this stage, we have no clear onward travel plans apart from wishing to visit the Temple of Isis and to continue creating the range of temple essences. Later Sahir calls to ask if we are happy about the voucher and offers us an amazing deal for a cruise along the Nile. Many travel bookings have been cancelled, so the boats have plenty of space and are looking to fill their cabins. We also ask Sahir to book a flight to Aswan and a hotel overlooking the river so we will have time to visit the temple. To finalise payment we must meet his boss at the travel agency.

Rashid is the owner of a successful tourism agency and a chain of up-market jewellery shops. He encourages me to try on elaborate pieces of jewellery, beautiful Isis necklaces and bracelets. He admires me wearing the different pieces, all way out of my price range. He seems very keen to get to know me and invites us for dinner at a restaurant overlooking the pyramids. Rashid also owns a papyrus art studio where we commission the painting of scrolls of the Egyptian chakra symbols to bring back for our students in Australia.

Over dinner, Rashid tells us he is divorced and would like to remarry soon. He constantly gazes into my eyes and then reaches over the table taking my hand to measure what ring size I would take if I were to accept his marriage proposal! I am stunned by this behaviour and grateful that Mary is with me. I feel curiously overwhelmed by Rashid's controlling attention. Later we laugh at this bizarre situation and look forward to leaving Cairo the next day.

I have a great feeling of freedom as the plane takes off for the next stage of our pilgrimage through the temples of Egypt. Both Mary and I have a strong calling to the Temple of Isis, which sits on an island in the sparkling waters of the Nile. This magnificent temple dates from the 4th century BCE and was the last temple in use for worshipping the Goddess Isis when the Roman Emperor, Justinian, closed it down in 551 CE.

In the early 20th century, due to the building of the Old Aswan Dam, the island of Philae was submerged for six months every year, so visitors viewed the underwater ruins from boats. In the 1960's with the prospect of the new High Dam construction, a rescue was organised by UNESCO to move the Temple complex stone by stone to a neighbouring island. This process took eight years to complete, and the temple was re-opened to the public in 1980. For centuries, pilgrims have come from all over the world to worship here. Excited to embark on this same journey, we are curious to feel if the Temple still carries the ancient wisdom of the Isis Mystery School in its new location.

In Aswan we stay at the beautiful Old Cataract Hotel, a

nineteenth century Victorian palace, overlooking the Nile at the edge of the Nubian Desert. This hotel became famous when the Agatha Christie movie, 'Death on the Nile', was filmed here. Luckily we have been advised by a friend to request a room in the older, traditional part, as there is also a contemporary tower block with the same name. The interior is an exquisite blend of Moorish arches, ruby-red chandeliers, plush Persian carpets and hand-carved furnishings of times gone by.

We enjoy delicious gelato on the terrace and are mesmerised by the view of the river, overlooking Elephanta Island, with the feluccas (traditional sailing boats) drifting by and the palm trees wafting gently in the breeze.

The next morning we eagerly make our way to the Temple of Isis. At the quay there are many boat operators waiting, so we bargain for a good price and are soon being transported across the river towards the island of Philae. As we are carried over the river, my heart centre is open. I take in the sunlight glimmering on the water and the gentle touch of the breeze on my face. I feel tranquil and calm, yet as the temple comes into view, a wave of emotion rises up, along with the familiar feeling of 'coming home' as I recall making this crossing in other lifetimes.

We reach the island and climb the steps to the courtyard in front of the enormous ceremonial gateway, carved with images of Isis, Horus and other deities. It feels as if time is slowing down as we retrace our steps and explore this magnificent temple. We walk with mindfulness along the vast colonnade of carved pillars bringing awareness to the consciousness in each step we take.

One of the temple guardians invites us into a small dimly lit room. He chants the mantra "Isis, Isis, Isis…" over and over again, then blesses us with a holy basil plant. However, we are following our intuitive connection with Isis and she guides us to make the essence out in the open in a small courtyard with a view of the original island of Philae, connecting the energies between the two sites. As we sit in meditation it is clear the sacred energy of the temple is carried within its stones and visiting this powerful site can activate cellular memories of ancient wisdom and invoke a sense of coming home to yourself.

One of the messages I receive here from Isis is "Remember you are an initiate of the Temple of Isis", and that I will meet a man who

I must remind that he too is an initiate of Isis. We spend many hours blissfully reconnecting with the energies of the Temple of Isis. This is my favourite temple of all the places we visit along the Nile. In my healing work I often meet people who have a strong calling to the Priestess Path; I feel a deep soul connection with them in this life and believe they are members of my soul family group.

Visiting the Temple of Philae activates my ancient memories as an initiate of the Goddess Isis. I remember that to follow the path of the Priestess is to live each day as a ritual, attuning my body with movement, song and dance. We walk with the Goddess, not striving to reach a goal, but being conscious in every action, acknowledging the seasons and the cycles of nature. Daily tasks are a simple celebration of life and an honouring of the natural world. My belief is that our physical body is a temple, a sacred place of ancient wisdom and when we choose to walk a conscious path, we have the opportunity to come home to ourselves.

We are sad to leave Aswan but looking forward to our Nile cruise. For the following week we travel down-river towards Luxor and the temple of the Sun God, Ra. We visit seven more temples and are offered unexpected openings in our quest to create the essences. Remarkably, we are often given access to the inner sanctuary, where few tourists are invited, perhaps because we are travelling alone and not as part of a group. My personal feeling is that we are being mysteriously blessed in our spiritual vocation.

Past Life Love Affair

During our trip, Sahir has been calling almost daily to check we are being well looked after. I begin to have longer conversations with him, sharing our experiences and laughing together. He offers to arrange accommodation for us when we arrive back in Cairo—in Zamalek on the island of Gezira. He is keen to meet me so, with Mary's encouragement; we agree the three of us will meet in Khan el-Khalili, the famous souk or Egyptian bazaar.

We enjoy an evening in a traditional Arabic coffee house where waiters serve refreshments, light the charcoal in the sweet smelling hookahs and musicians sing along to the sound of the oud. We have fun shopping in the labyrinth of colourful alleyways for souvenirs, jewellery, papyrus paintings and appreciate the assistance of a local to help with our bargaining negotiations.

Sahir is tall, dark haired and good looking. Our attraction is mutual. We begin a brief and passionate holiday romance in the privacy of our hotel room. Our lovemaking has a familiar intimacy, a unique sweetness, and when he speaks the words "Habibi, habibi…" (my darling) my heart melts.

During the day, Sahir either goes to work or stays in the hotel. He refuses to be seen out in public with me in case his boss, Rashid, happens to see him, as he would lose his job. Meanwhile, Rashid has been constantly calling, wanting to meet with me again. I would prefer to avoid this, but would like to get the papyrus paintings we have already paid for. Mary and I eventually meet with him in a busy hotel coffee shop and, much to his disappointment, tell him we are about to leave town.

During this time I have a strong past-life memory:

I am living in Cairo with my family who are very poor. I am a teenage girl, very beautiful and I know that I will be sold in marriage to make money for my family. My mother tells me I will be treated 'like a princess' by my husband. However, I am sad that I cannot marry the man I truly love.

Following my marriage, I am locked away behind closed doors, surrounded by beautiful things. My clothes and veils are edged with gold and I wear ornate jewellery. I have many riches, but my husband does not love me. He only wants me for my beauty.

After some time, my beloved comes to rescue me and we run away, through the streets of Cairo at night to be safe together in each other's arms. Yet we must live in secret and in the fear of being punished for our deeds. Our love is so sweet, each night we gain the strength to live this secret life.

I eventually put two and two together and realise this past life saga has played out again in this lifetime between Rashid, Sahir and myself. Rashid is the 'controlling' male who thinks he can buy me with beautiful jewellery and Sahir is the love I ran away to be with in secret. In an uncanny replay of the story, we cannot walk the streets together in daylight for fear of being discovered and punished. Once more our romantic nights together are intimate, sweet and loving.

Egypt has its own caste system and Sahir is from the lower class, he believes there will never be the opportunity for him to advance his status in life. However, when we do a spiritual healing with him, it is clear that he too was once an initiate of the Goddess Isis and that if he draws on this memory and aligns himself with the quality of worthiness, he will become more successful in his career. Some years later I hear that he has advanced in the travel industry and relocated to Dubai as an Egyptian tourism manager.

When the time comes to leave Egypt, Mary and I feel satisfied and complete in our spiritual mission. We carefully carry the seven mother tinctures home in our hand luggage in a cool bag. At this point passengers are still allowed to carry liquids onto the plane in Cairo, but we anticipate being questioned on arrival in Sydney. When the customs officer greets us, she asks where we are coming from and hearing we have travelled from Egypt says "I bet you're really glad to be home! Welcome back, go straight through."

Healing Inspiration from the Great Pyramid – Throat Chakra

❖ Appreciating the Power of Words and the Sacredness of Silence

The throat chakra (Vishuddhi) is the primary centre of communication and creative expression. Finding a balance between constant verbal communication and times of silence is essential when wishing to hear and understand your own inner guidance. Trusting the intuitive messages you receive takes practice as does making the time to be in silence. Setting up a regular time for mediation enhances your ability to go within, find inner silence and hear your own guidance. Just five or ten minutes can make a real difference.

Meditation is the most effective way to still our minds and access our intuition. This instinctive connection often occurs when we spend time in nature, being creative or completing simple tasks, such as gardening. A moving meditation, walking in silence with conscious awareness of each step, is a simple and beautiful way to begin a mindfulness practice.

Focus on your throat centre and become aware of the balance between speaking and maintaining silence. Observe the words you speak and what you choose to keep to yourself. This simple meditation clears the throat chakra and brings clarity:

Sitting quietly with your eyes closed, notice your breathing and observe the gentle movement of the breath flowing in and out. With each exhalation, allow yourself to relax into your body a little deeper. Now bring your awareness to the throat centre and imagine a small blue candle flame here, deep within your throat. Find the centre of the flame and breathe into this point, feeling the breath flowing into your throat. Visualise the candle flame glowing brighter as you exhale – this purifying flame will clear and balance your throat chakra. Complete at least seven breaths focusing on the blue flame and feeling your throat relax. From this place of stillness, imagine a word appears from within the flame. See the letters of the word in front of you and reflect on what it means to you. Trust that your intuition will guide you, even if you do not know the literal meaning. You may want to write the word down and explore its meaning further.

- ❖ **Listening to the Wisdom of Mother Earth**

    Many traditional cultures, including the ancient Egyptians, believed the Earth to be a living, breathing creature of the universe, with all forms of life being interconnected. In Egypt, the earth was worshipped as the God Geb, the stars and the night sky as the Goddess Nut who rebirthed the sun (the God Ra) each morning. The Goddess Isis, the Divine Mother, daughter of Geb and Nut, was married to the Osiris (God of the Underworld and the Afterlife). In death, the Goddess Maat (Mother of the Underworld), would weigh the heart against a feather to check for heaviness, a lightness of heart indicated a life of integrity and honesty.

    The Priestesses of Egypt connected with the cycles of nature and conducted rituals and ceremonies in honour and respect of the natural world. This is a powerful custom we can continue in present time, either through spiritual intention or by participating in activities that increase awareness of the harmful practices that do not benefit the future of the planet.

    Conducting simple gratitude rituals in everyday life helps us to stay grounded and raises our consciousness to a higher vibration. Setting up a simple nature altar in your home or garden is a way to focus positive energy and call on the support of the Divine Mother. Select meaningful objects or symbols to represent the qualities you would like to invite into your life and place them where you can see them as you go about daily tasks.

    A short video on Creating Chakra Altars is available on the Spirit Way website. ₄

❖ ***Enjoying Sound and Music for Planetary Healing***
The vibration of sound is recognised as a powerful healing modality in its own right. In many cultures, sound has been used as a 'call to prayer' or to signify the beginning of rituals and ceremonies. The deep resonance of the conch shell in Buddhist and Hindu traditions vibrates through our auric field. The Tibetan singing bowls clear and balance our chakras and the playing of the Oud carries us back to times gone by.

Listening to, or playing music, is a natural way to express yourself. Enjoy singing or dancing to your favourite musicians. Chanting (kirtan) with a group, or simply toning alone (allowing a natural sound to emanate from deep within) are joyful and powerful ways to offer prayers for peace to Mother Earth.

Great Pyramid, Egypt – Historical Facts

Situated on the Giza Plateau on the outskirts of Cairo, the Great Pyramid is the oldest of the Seven Wonders of the ancient world. It was built to a perfect geometrical structure over a 10–20 year period and completed around 2560 BCE. The Sphinx sits as its guardian, looking out over the desert. Within the pyramid is an enormous stairway, the Great Gallery, ascending to the King's Chamber or burial chamber, an area never intended to be seen by the public.

Chapter 4

Heart Chakra

Chalice Well, Glastonbury, England

Sacred Union Within and Without

During a healing session:
I find an aspect of my inner feminine lying in the bottom of a deep lake. She has been there for some time, lying there stuck in the mud. She represents the feminine part of my self who does not trust the masculine. She is afraid of betrayal and of never being in a loving partnership again, even though her heart is open to giving and receiving love.

As I reconnect with this wounded aspect of my inner feminine, I initially feel immobilised and unable to release myself from the mud. I am reminded of the lotus flower, which has its roots deeply anchored in the mud, before rising tall and blossoming. The healing waters of the lake support me in naming and releasing the old beliefs that have prevented me from feeling safe to open my heart to a man who can be fully present with me in loving relationship. As these distorted beliefs release from my heart chakra, I feel myself floating to the surface of the lake where the blue lotus flower blooms.

Floating gently in the healing waters, I begin to feel more negative patterns arising in me, this time relating to my family of origin, and the matriarchal line of women who have all felt betrayed by men. I remember my mother, my grandmother and her mother before her, all carrying the pain of this pattern. I call on the healing angels to assist in releasing it, and pray for the restoration to flow back down the line of seven generations of women to rebuild trust and balance in male-female relating. I ask for the healing to flow forward to the next seven generations of women, including my daughters, so they may enjoy loving harmonious relationships.

The soft scent of the blue lotus surrounds me as I breathe into my heart centre, feeling myself coming back into a joyful, expansive and loving space. I now feel ready to emerge from the healing waters of the lake and walk slowly through the surrounding landscape to the foot of the Tor in Glastonbury. I become aware of the loving male energy of my inner masculine by my side and together we ascend the hill and enter St Michael's tower at the top.

We stand close, facing each other in an expression of balanced masculine-feminine in divine union. We connect our heart chakras with an infinity flow of emerald green light joining our inner heart flames. The Archangels, Michael, Uriel, Gabrielle and Ariel, surround us offering their unconditional love. As we raise our hands to the heavens, we are blessed with golden light showering down from above; I hear the words "You are now ready for love".

Healing My Heart

My mother gave birth to me at home in Sherwood, Nottingham. Homebirth was a common and natural event in England in the late fifties, where each village had a community midwife attending the women in her local area. The labour progressed normally, with my mother's sister and my grandmother in attendance, along with the midwife. When mum shared my birth story with me, she said the second stage of labour (moving me down through the birth canal) took some time. Thankfully, time was not an issue as no-one was in a hurry, and I slowly emerged into the familiar surroundings of home. Mum was able to rest well and be cared for by the family as she recovered and established breastfeeding.

Homebirth continues to be well supported in England today, and women can choose to birth at home with a midwife on the National Health Service. This is dramatically different to Australia and America, where pregnant women choosing to give birth at home have to engage and pay for a private midwife themselves.

I believe my own natural birth and arrival into the world has had a positive cellular imprint on my beliefs about birth and my passion for supporting pregnant and birthing women to connect with their own inner strength and trust to birth their babies naturally. My 'inner birthing calling' was re-activated by the empowering homebirth of my first daughter, Jade, and strengthened by the calm home water birth of her sister, Amber, nineteen months later. Both births were wonderful experiences that completely transformed my life.

When I was four years old, my sister was born and, apart from the usual 'first born' feelings of being displaced as the only child, we gradually formed a strong sisterly bond. I do recall wanting to tip Jane out of her pram soon after she arrived and feeling envious of all the attention she received with her soft, white blonde hair and cuteness, but it was all pretty normal sibling rivalry.

As a small child I recall the different homes we lived in. Dad was on a career path that meant changing location every couple of years, so we got used to moving around. Most of my memories involve the subtle smells, sounds and environment of the different places, especially the gardens. At one stage, my father was the Station Master in Newcastle-under-Lyne and we lived in the station house, which had a large garden backing onto the railway track. From the edge of the garden I could see the railway signals changing to indicate the arrival of the next train. Mum said I would spend hours letting her know what was about to happen down the track. Even today I find the sound of a train moving rhythmically over the track comforting.

Most of our travel in those days was taken on the train using the free pass that came with Dad's job. Later on, we began to use the car more often. However, before I turned eighteen, Mum insisted on taking Jane and me to Paris on the train and ferry, before I would lose my eligibility for the free travel. At the time, I was amazed at how easily Mum navigated being in a foreign country and guiding us around the beautiful city. Looking back I realise my parents had done plenty of travel in Europe before I arrived. They even honeymooned in Spain, which was very exotic in those days! Perhaps this is partly where my own love of travel came from and my parents were always very encouraging and excited for me whenever I mentioned a trip to a new country.

During our childhood, we went on many lovely summer holidays, including Scotland, where we played naked in a mountain stream. We both remember the feeling of the warm sunlight on our bodies and the feeling of freedom in this simple pleasure. We also had several beautiful summers down in Cornwall near Treyarnon Bay, where we played for hours in the rock pools. Dad would enjoy swimming in the ocean whilst Mum got a suntan. They were both happily relaxed, holding hands and being affectionate with each other.

Around Nottingham there were plenty of parks and rural areas. One of the memorable places we visited often was Sherwood Forest, of Robin Hood fame, where we played hide and seek in the trees and made up games. We ran around the Major Oak Tree, the legendary tree where Robin Hood and his merry men were said to have hidden inside its hollow trunk. Amazingly this tree, estimated to be between 800 and 1000 years old, is still standing today, sadly now supported by timber scaffolding. Over the years on my visits back to England, I would walk in the bluebell carpeted parkland and enjoy the natural smells and sounds of my childhood.

The nature in England is much softer than here in Australia. The seasons are more clearly defined, especially the gentle re-emergence in the springtime when the blossoms begin to bloom. I remember lying on the soft lawn surrounded by daisies and buttercups, making daisy chains and playing with newly-mown grass cuttings. By comparison, nature Down Under can feel unforgiving under the harshness of the Australian sun. This tenderness of the natural world where I grew up is one of the few things I miss about England.

When I was eleven years old, an unexpected event happened, that changed my whole belief system about love and relationships, and affected my ability to trust men. My father began an affair with another woman. This affair would last seven years until I was eighteen. I cannot remember at exactly what point my mother began to confide in me about her experience of this betrayal—perhaps I was twelve and just at the threshold of becoming a woman. Looking back, I was far too young to handle her intimate sharing and felt responsible for the disconnection and conflict between my parents. I would later spend many years unpacking and healing my need to be the responsible one in many situations, which is also a typical trait carried by a child of an alcoholic family.

There were many evenings when Dad would arrive home late in a drunken state. Mum would be waiting up for him and I would hear them begin to argue loudly downstairs. On several occasions, I got out of bed and tried to intervene, wishing to protect my mother from the verbal abuse. This often resulted in a slanging match of verbal abuse, with me taking sides with Mum and feeling powerless to resolve the situation. I now understand my father was in the early stages of alcoholism and his behaviour was spiralling out of control.

When the affair finally ended, with the 'other woman' leaving Dad for another man, my parents just carried on with married life. They did not talk about the situation. Neither did they undertake any counselling or appear to come to any new resolution about their relationship. They tried to put the episode behind them and carry on, although Mum continued to express her resentment and frustration about it until the day she died—confiding in Jane and me, usually when we were out walking the dog.

My mother was one of seven children. She had two sisters and three brothers. Their own father (my grandfather) had left my grandmother to bring up the children on her own. We never met our grandfather. I remember hearing negative comments about him between my mother and my aunties. He paid my grandmother a fortnightly 'maintenance' payment of approximately two shillings and six pence! Occasionally this payment was late and my mother would wonder if her father had died. The children never re-established a relationship with him, nor did they openly express any grief about the loss of their father. In England after the war, everyone just 'got on with it' with a stiff upper lip—thus began the pattern of pushing down confronting emotions.

My parents had been married for twenty years before the affair and a favourite saying of Mum's was "Well we had twenty happy years!" She said this in a way that seemed to express "I've had more love than I deserved". They were married in their early twenties, after being schoolyard sweethearts, and were together for a total of 56 years, so there were many more years after the affair where she still carried the bitterness and resentment of Dad's betrayal. At the time of Mum's death, Dad expressed "I've always loved your mother, apart from one small indiscretion." For me that small seven-year indiscretion shaped my future relationships. Healing my own heart from this wound of betrayal was a significant theme on my healing journey to accept that I was loveable.

My early relationships were unfulfilling, including a five-year relationship with an older married man, which began when I was just eighteen. Of course, I never intended to go into relationship with a man who was already committed, but I now realise it was a desperate attempt to feel loved, fuelled by the desire to replace the love I thought I had lost from my father. I tried to end this relationship many times, but my attachment and the constant reassurance of his love and intention to be with me, kept me tied to him. I believed if I kept on loving him unconditionally, we would eventually be together. The unhealthy pattern of not deserving love from men was clearly established in my belief system during this time.

I finally broke away from this toxic bond, yet continued throughout my twenties to have relationships with men who were emotionally unavailable, until I met James when I was thirty, and just about to migrate to Australia. I already had a job to go to in Sydney, however my visa was delayed for a month longer than expected and it was during this time James and I fell in love.

James adored me, in fact, it was the first time a man had really put me on a pedestal and I felt completely loved and respected. The fact that I was a successful businesswoman at the time did not put James off. It was the complete opposite. He embraced my busy, high profile career and social life and became the pillar of strength at my side that I had been longing for. When I left England, neither of us were ready to make a commitment, so we began a long-distance courtship with handwritten letters and enormous phone bills. After six long months, James came to Australia. He loved the country and we were in love. We had a magical holiday together visiting the city, mountains, sea, islands and the Great Barrier Reef.

A clairvoyant once told me I would 'marry a man from overseas'. I assumed she meant a man from an exotic foreign country, like Africa, South America or the Pacific Islands. It turned out to be a man from England who would travel overseas to be with me in Australia! James arrived in Sydney one year and one day after me. He came with a marriage visa that stated we needed to marry within six weeks of his arrival. We were ecstatic to finally be together and joyfully prepared for our wedding at Whale Beach on the Northern Beaches of Sydney.

I am eternally grateful for the love and support James provided in our early years together. He was a 'hands-on' dad to our beautiful daughters and our relationship lasted over twelve years. I know that during this time, I was changing and becoming more immersed in following my spiritual path, teaching yoga, meditation, sacred birth and healing. James tried hard to embrace this path with me, however, being on a pedestal is very precarious and we eventually went our separate ways.

The family pattern of alcoholism was clearly embedded in my psyche from my own childhood and I found it more and more difficult to be around this addictive 'drug', even though I still enjoyed a G & T or glass of wine myself at the time. Funnily enough, one of my later significant love relationships was with a Drug and Alcohol Counsellor! Nowadays, I prefer not to drink alcohol, and this happened naturally. The more I worked with the spiritual realm, the more alcohol just dropped away. It was not difficult to let it go and I feel clearer, more connected, vital and present now.

Drinking from the Chalice Well

Glastonbury was calling me. I travelled back to England many times, as my parents were aging and needing greater care. Each time I tried to make the space to visit the Chalice Well and the home of the Goddess Temple. Finally in 2001 this happened. I left my parent's place a week before flying back to Australia and drove through the English countryside down to Glastonbury. Although I had been there several times in my twenties to attend the well-known music festival, this was a pilgrimage of a very different kind.

Before I left, a most unexpected healing with my father occurred. I have always found it difficult to share with him about my birth and spiritual work. He was very proud of my success in the business world and had little understanding as to why I did not continue on that more financially rewarding path. On this visit, I had a set of my recently published *'Birthing the Spirit'* cards with me and I was hesitant to show them to him, feeling sensitive in case he was critical of this 'out there' idea. On the last day, I plucked up the courage to share my 'baby' with him and he spent some time looking at the cards and reading through the accompanying book. Just as I was leaving for Glastonbury, he picked up the first card entitled *Love Ritual—*, referring to the conscious conception of a baby. He held the card up to me and said in his beautiful, deep voice *"May the*

Force Be with You!"

These simple words of affirmation were the response I had longed for; I now felt seen and acknowledged by my father in my spiritual vocation.

Temple of the Goddess

Driving through the countryside, I felt blessed and free to be on the right path. I enjoyed the scenery, passing through vibrant green hills and freshly-mown meadows. The smell of summer was in the air. Arriving at the small town of Glastonbury is rather like entering a different reality—much like the fairy tale mystery surrounding the sacred Isle of Avalon. The small streets are filled with New Age shops and posters advertising local gatherings, pagan rituals and seasonal ceremonies. Much to my relief, there were plenty of vegetarian and wholefood cafes.

Central to the New Age and medieval influences are both the Abbey, where it is said that King Arthur was buried beside his lovely wife, Queen Guinevere, and the Goddess Temple, which celebrates the presence of the Divine Feminine with these words:

> *THE GODDESS is alive in Glastonbury, visible for all to see in the shapes of the sacred landscape.*
> *She is soft as the rounded hills of Her body and sweet as the apple blossom that grows in Her orchards.*
>
> *Here Her love enfolds us every day and Her voice is always near, carried on the wind, whispering through the mists of Avalon.*
> *Her Mysteries are as deep as the Cauldron She stirs, taking us down into Her depths and lifting us up to Her heights.*
> *She is our Source, our Inspiration and our Love.*

I feel immediately at home here and eagerly begin exploring the town, looking for the perfect place to stay. One of the flyers that caught my eye is for the Shambhala Retreat, run by a fascinating couple named Isis and Akhenaten. Isis is the name of the Egyptian

Goddess and Akhenaten an Egyptian Pharaoh, married to Nefertiti, who tried to bring about a departure from the traditional religion and the worship of different Gods and Goddesses, to only worshipping one God. However, the retreat centre offers organic vegetarian food and treatments for 'mind, body and spirit' and does sound appealing.

My comfortable bedroom, the Dove Room, faces the lovely garden and the coop where the doves gently coo. I settle into meditation, connecting with the energies of Avalon, where two powerful ley lines cross in three places, known as the masculine Michael Line and the feminine Mary Line. Sitting or standing on these spots can bring a feeling of balance and peace.

I ask for guidance from my spirit guides and my higher self to support my sacred work for the healing of the planet and for loving relationships between all Beings. I call upon the Goddess to assist me to be balanced in my own heart centre before making the essence for the planetary Heart Chakra. In meditation I connect with my inner feminine and inner masculine energies.

> *I see myself beside a lake. I dive down into the depths of the lake and enter through the doors of the Temple of my Heart. There is a beautiful altar with two candle flames burning brightly, where my inner female and inner male stand facing each other. My feminine self appears as a beautiful maiden with long silky hair and a flowing white dress. However, she feels quite rigid and stuck in the place where she stands. My masculine self gazes into her eyes, but when I try to connect with his feelings, he appears to grow very small and miniature in size, in fact so tiny that he can stand in the palm of my female's hand. I now see he is feeling rejected and not welcomed by my female self.*
>
> *I ask for balance and healing for my heart, and as I do this, my inner feminine becomes more flowing and open, inviting my male self into her space. As this happens, my male seems to grow taller again, until he is gazing into her eyes as her equal. I go through a process of forgiveness between my inner selves "Surrendering all that I am in relationship with you... forgiving, releasing and rebuilding our relationship together". We say these words three times to each other, trusting in divine law. Our heart chakras now*

connect with golden light in a figure of eight, infinity flow, radiating the love of our sacred marriage between us and throughout the temple.

Early the next morning, I begin my climb to the top of the Glastonbury Tor, which can be seen from a great distance rising above the flat plains of the Summerland meadows. The Tor is a conical hill that forms a right angle triangle between the sacred sites of Avebury and Stonehenge. There are many myths and legends related to the Tor. One is that it is home to Gwyn ap Nudd, the Lord of the Underworld, and a place where the fairy folk live. There is also some evidence that the terracing on the slopes of Glastonbury Tor is the remains of a three-dimensional Neolithic labyrinth, a ceremonial way dedicated to the ancient Goddess. For this reason many thousands of pilgrims have walked it in a sacred manner.

I take the path that leads from the retreat centre to the back of the Tor, walking down Gypsy and Basketfield Lanes, through the kissing gate and there it stands, right in front of me. I have no idea that there is a path leading up to the top of the Tor just around the other side so I begin to climb directly up the grassy bank and this is where my contemplative sacred walk comes to an end. The ground is wet and I am scrabbling to keep my footing, slipping and sliding and trying to hold on to tufts of grass.

I reach the top out of breath and frazzled, not exactly 'Priestess-like'! Of course, as soon as I see the easier route with paved walkway from the front approach, I have to laugh at myself... I could view my difficult climb as an initiation through the mists of Avalon, but sometimes it just pays to get a map before you start.

The scene from the top of the Tor is mystical. It is early summer and the new morning light softly lights up the landscape. The magnificent view takes in the Somerset Levels, Dorset, Wiltshire and Wales. The surrounding low-lying ground can produce a visual effect known as a Fata Morgana when the Tor appears to rise out of the mist. The Italian term Fata Morgana is derived from the name of Morgan le Fey, the powerful sorceress in Arthurian legend.

I think I am alone as I enter St Michael's Chapel on top of the Tor. The climb was worth it and I settle down, taking in the enchanting view, beginning to meditate. Suddenly the sound of music floats through the air, and I realise there is a man sitting in the grass playing the flute. As I relax, the musical notes seem to pour through me like a waterfall, coming to rest in my heart centre.

The timeless sound of the flute carries me away to distant times and memories of a past life as a Priestess of Avalon—a time when I worked with herbs and tinctures, creating alchemy and celebrating my intuitive and healing gifts—a time when I followed the path of the Goddess.

My heart chakra is now gently open and I feel peaceful as I return to the retreat centre in time for breakfast. The group of guests are mostly from other parts of the country and it is their first visit to Glastonbury. We enjoy a delicious breakfast and then Isis announces, in a rather school teacher-like manner, "Right, we are now going to have the heart-opening meditation". We duly follow her outside into the garden where there is a beautiful star-shaped mosaic on the patio. Some of the women look a little nervous. I know how to stay grounded, but am also aware and protective of my own inner-heart process. We stand in a circle and Isis leads a meditation encouraging us all to 'open our heart chakras wide'. She then adds if anyone is having difficulty with this process, they may wish to book a personal session with Akhenaten, before we are released to enjoy the day. I decide to stay somewhere else the next night, as I am deeply immersed in my own spiritual quest and prefer to align with my own guidance.

As a spiritual teacher myself, I am always sensitive to each person's individual process and endeavour to ensure my healing energy is in affinity with another's ability to receive and process transformational changes in present time. This protectiveness feels justified when, later that afternoon, I bump into one of the women in a café, and she confides her session with Akhenaten has stirred up dormant childhood emotions that she does not know how to deal with. I listen as she lets the tears flow, and then help her to ground and reconnect with her spirit again. It pays to be discerning when visiting new places and to ensure there is follow-up support when we choose to dive into our past hurts or trauma. As with all the chakra sites around the world, Glastonbury is a place of transformation and simply being in this place of power can bring about significant healing and clarity on one's life path.

The Chalice Well gardens and orchards are a living sanctuary, the home of one of the most ancient and well-loved wells in Britain, nestled in the Vale of Avalon between the Tor and Chalice Hill. The Chalice Well Trust holds regular events of celebration, marking the *wheel of the year* with meditation, poetry and performance throughout the summer months in the candlelit gardens.

I walk through the gardens absorbing the serenity, abundance of flowers, the sweet bird song and peaceful surroundings. There is a feeling of life bursting forth and magic in the air here. I spend the day wandering through the delightful grounds, sitting under one of the guardian yew trees and meditating to the sound of the waterfall. I ground my roots deeply into the earth here in the land of my birth, and open my heart to the spirit of the trees and plants, connecting with the nature devas (spirits of the forest) present here. Then I bathe my feet in the healing pool, symbolically cleansing and purifying myself—ready to create the essence—and drink the iron-rich healing water from the Lion's Head Fountain.

The waters of the Chalice Well have many legends. They are acknowledged as the essence of life, gift from Mother Earth, a continuous spring that is a direct expression of unbounded life force. Another firm belief is that the holy waters represent the blood of Christ miraculously springing forth from the ground when Joseph of Arimathea buried or washed the Holy Chalice used at the Last Supper.

The cover of the well features a wrought iron symbol, the Vesica Piscis, an ancient symbol of two identical interlocking circles, with a lance passing through the middle. This sacred geometry symbolises a union of heaven and earth, or spirit and matter. For me it also represents the symbol of sacred marriage, both inner and outer union.

After several hours in the gardens, I am feeling content and tranquil with a peaceful heart. I decide the essence will be created tomorrow morning, using the holy waters and connecting to the divine life flow energy of the Chalice Well. Now I need to find a new place to stay… this proves to be easy, the first New Age shop I walk into has a brochure for a healing centre that offers the Aura-Soma Colour Therapy and each room is decorated in one of the colours from the Aura-Soma range. I am given the lovely blue room and it complements the tranquillity I am already feeling.

The next morning I awaken early to meditate, feeling my heart chakra becoming a golden chalice, with the stem of the goblet connecting me to the earth through my lower chakras. The energy of unconditional divine love pours in to fill the chalice from above as I ask for guidance from my spirit guides and my higher self to support my sacred work for the healing of the planet and for loving relationships between all Beings. I call upon the Goddess:

> **Divine Goddess, Holy, Mother, Keeper of Truth**
> *"I bless thee and thank thee. I ask that you charge me with your wisdom and healing that I may do this work in purity and truth with the clarity to bestow your blessings on this planet and to those who walk its sacred ground in beauty."*

In quiet solitude I enter the Gateway to the Chalice Well gardens. I have chosen to place the glass dish right next to the Well, protected by my two crystal guardians, I sit in the warm sun on a nearby bench to set the energy and call in divine blessings for the essence. I am deep in meditation, when a young couple dressed in medieval clothing come to the well. They have come to partake of the water and to perform their own simple love ritual. They are glowing and gaze at each other adoringly. I watch respectfully as the two of them whisper words of love to each other, embracing and tying ribbons on to the nearby wishing tree. This is the perfect energetic blessing of pure love and sacred union for the essence of the planetary Heart Chakra. I am filled with gratitude, and in my own heart centre, my inner feminine and masculine aspects are dancing together.

When I return to Australia, I continue to carry the powerful energies of the Chalice Well and, when giving healing sessions, this divine love flows through me to others. I am compelled to draw the beautiful imagery I see flowing into each person's aura. These drawings all contain a chalice, but each has unique colours and light pouring in, filling the heart chakra with the essence of the Goddess.

The Cycles of Life

My years of traveling back and forth to England were coming to a close as my parents neared the end of their lives. In her later years, my mother developed Alzheimer's, the form of dementia that robs a person of their memory and, in particular, their short-term memories. During these years, each time Jane or I would visit, Mum seemed to be a little worse, until it became more like trying to communicate with a small child. On occasions, Mum would have conversations with me that I did not understand. Then I would realise she believed I was one of her sisters and was talking about an event from her childhood. I stopped correcting her and just let the conversation flow as if I was the person she was talking to at the time. At other times her memory would be clear and she would recognise and talk to me as myself.

It was during one of these present-time conversations, and after my own marriage break-up, that Mum quite innocently asked me *"Did you know your Dad had an affair?"* This question stunned me for a while, and then I just had to laugh at the ridiculousness of life and all the years I had spent processing the stories she had confided in me. This innocent question somehow let me 'off the hook' and I felt a sense of release and relief that I no longer had to carry around this emotional baggage that Mum could not even remember!

Nowadays, I can see the gift in all those years of listening to my mother as preparation for my work today supporting women at emotional times of transformation in their lives. I also believe, on another level, that I had a soul contract with Mum to support her through those years when she had no-one else to talk to during that stressful time.

Even though Jane and I lived twelve thousand miles away, we were thankful to be in England at the time of both our parent's deaths. In 2007, Mum had been hospitalised, as Dad was not capable of looking after her any longer. She had gotten into the habit of refusing to eat and had become so dehydrated that the doctor insisted she receive care. At this time Dad was also on oxygen for emphysema. He had been a smoker all his life and could barely walk. He was unable to leave the house to visit the hospital. It became clear that Mum was in her last weeks of life, so, with the support of the family doctor; I arranged to bring her home, where Jane and I could care for her.

Mum took her last breath a few days later. As I sat beside her bed during the last hours, I connected with her spirit and saw clairvoyantly that her chakras were closing down as her spirit prepared to leave her body. The chakra she was still strongly attached to was the heart centre. I prayed that the final release from her physical body would be easy. A little later, the phone rang with a call from my dear friend, Kaliana Rose, in Australia. Kaliana is an intuitive and sound healer who has developed a beautiful range of healing mantras for the chakras and she reminded me of the mantra for the heart.

Together Jane and I sang this mantra to Mum and asked for her transition to be grace filled. A short time later, she took her last breath. Through our tears, we bathed her and honoured the physical body of our mother, who had given birth to us, fed us, nourished and always encouraged us to follow our dreams. Dad sat with her for a very long time saying his good-byes, which would not have been possible if she had been in hospital.

I have attended many births as a doula (support person), and now I have the personal experience of the intimate connection between the portals of birth and death. The same light-filled presence fills the room in birth and in death. Mum's spirit was now expansive and free. Together we planned the funeral, chose flowers in Mum's favourite colours and dealt with all the necessary paperwork.

On our walks in the nearby park, we felt her presence in the trees, the birds and the sky. We scattered her ashes in this place where she had spent countless hours walking the dog, laughing at Bonnie's antics as she got covered in mud at the edge of the lake. Carpets of bluebells in the woodlands will always remind me of this sacred time.

Sadly, we both had to return to Australia after a few weeks. Before leaving, we arranged on-going care for Dad, who had begun to feel sorry for himself now that he was alone and wished he been the first one to die.

There is a condition called broken heart syndrome, believed to occur when someone loses a close partner or spouse. Death of a loved one is one of the most stressful things that can happen to a person. It has now been scientifically shown that the mental anguish and grief also has a physical component, these physical ailments can be very serious, directly affecting the heart.

The following two years were stressful for both Jane and me. We were grieving and Jane, in particular, felt guilty about living so far away. It is never easy staying connected to family when we choose to live in another country, so we worked out a plan to take it in turns to visit. We knew that Dad would turn to the most accessible means of comfort in his grief, the wine in which he could drown his sorrows and numb his feelings. This just made it more difficult to accept our powerlessness to change his behaviour. Ultimately it is this acceptance that sets a child of an alcoholic free.

Just before my fiftieth birthday, I spent time with Dad again. It had become more and more difficult to hold a conversation with him once he began drinking each day and this had now crept back to around eleven o'clock in the morning. He felt ready to die and expressed this clearly. He saw no point in living a housebound life where he was kept alive by medication. So, although he was grateful to have me around, it was clear the alcohol took priority.

I could occasionally still engage him in stories of travel. Tales of his time in the RAF after the war was a particular favourite. A time when he was commissioned with a small team of officers to conduct test flights over Africa, trying out aircraft to see how they performed in different conditions. He enthusiastically shared memories of flying high above Lake Victoria and over Mount Kilimanjaro. Dad greatly enjoyed the time spent in Africa, including Kenya, so this was a mutual love we shared.

Less than six weeks after returning to Australia, I received a call that Dad was in hospital. He had fallen and used the emergency button to call the ambulance. Even though he had been in hospital on a number of occasions, this time I felt the strong impulse to quickly return to England. At the time I was in a relationship with an astrologer, who checked Dad's astrology chart and saw an aspect indicating he could be close to death. Jane was unsure about coming straight away, but at the last minute changed her mind, so we booked flights together.

We arrived at the hospital in the afternoon, exhausted with jetlag and the long drive to Yorkshire. The nurses were relieved to see us and showed us into the small room where Dad lay hooked up to IV drips. We had a short visit together and then headed home to get some sleep. We had no idea how long we expected to be staying this time.

The next morning things moved quickly. The specialist caring for Dad came on his rounds while we were visiting. He could see Dad was exhausted and had had enough of being alive. "Now then Frederick" he said, "We can keep doing what we're doing or we can just make you comfortable." Dad respected this direct approach and responded clearly, "I'll choose the latter, doctor".

I became aware that Dad's spirit had already left his physical body with the exception of his crown chakra. He had such a strong intellect; this conscious decision to end his life was what was needed to release him fully and completely. Once this decision was made, Dad made sure Jane and I knew where all the important papers were: the will and the spare house key, efficiently taking care of all the last-minute details.

He then turned to us and lovingly expressed how grateful he was to have us in his life, saying the words I will always remember, "You have both given your Mum and I so much pleasure". We too shared our love for him and he then fell into a peaceful sleep. We sat beside him for some time before leaving the room briefly to get something to eat.

No sooner had we sat down in the cafeteria when a nurse came to find us as Dad was taking his last breaths. Often when people are in the final stages of dying, the family sit vigilantly at their bedside, this loving presence holds them in the physical realm. As the nurse shared, it is quite common for death to occur when the loved ones leave the room and this is what Dad's spirit chose.

We felt as if we were in a daze and were shocked at how quickly this all happened. Obviously Dad had been waiting for us to arrive from Australia to complete his business on earth. Our tears flowed as we said our goodbyes, and Jane shared a lovely meditation of the Rainbow Ritual. We connected with spiritual healing energy and wrapped Dad's physical body in rainbow colours of light with these words:

> *We wrap you in red - the colour of tomatoes and roses.*
> *We wrap you in orange – the colour of oranges, marigolds and nasturtiums.*
> *We wrap you in yellow – the colour of daffodils and warm golden sunshine.*
> *We wrap you in green – the colour of spring leaves and newly mown grass.*
> *We wrap you in blue – the colour of the clear blue sky and the calm ocean.*
> *We wrap you in indigo – the colour of the night sky behind the stars.*

> *We wrap you in violet – the colour of the sweet smelling flowers in the garden.*
> Petrea King, Quest for Life Foundation

Just as Dad would have wished, his funeral was an uplifting event and celebration of his life. Before he died, he had even made sure the freezer was stocked with the best Scottish salmon and Angus beef, as well as plenty of good wine. We felt his spirit smiling, as the words to one of his favourite Frank Sinatra songs resounded through the crematorium, *"Come fly with me, let's fly, let's fly away."*

We scattered Dad's ashes together with Mum's around the trees and the lake. His death marked the end of an era for me, and my connection with England was almost complete. The next two years were difficult, we were dealing with our grief and trying to finalise the sale of the home in England at a distance.

When this was settled, it was a huge relief. I could now focus on my life in Australia, where I had been a permanent resident and citizen for over twenty years. It is the vast landscapes, the pristine beaches, the lush rainforests and wide open roads that now call me home from my travels wherever I am in the world. They say home is where the heart is, and my heart truly resonates with the vibration of this ancient land.

Healing Inspiration from Glastonbury – Heart Chakra

❖ Healing the Heart Chakra – Sacred Marriage

Love is the foundation of all relationships and especially our relationship with our selves. All of our relationships are a reflection of the self. The love we receive reflects what we give out, and in the same way, all that is not love is a mirror of the inner hurts or wounds we carry from our past. When we are able to forgive past experiences and come to loving ourselves, we are truly ready to enter into sacred relationship with another.

A powerful way to bring balance in the heart chakra (Anahata) is to connect with your inner masculine and feminine aspects. Take the time to explore your inner Heart Temple and meet with these aspects of yourself to receive insights and guidance.

Sitting quietly, with eyes closed, allow your breath to wash over you like waves of relaxation and calm. Now visualise yourself diving deep into your personal Heart Temple. You enter through a pair of ornate doors and come to stand in front of the altar where there are two candles burning brightly. These candles represent your inner feminine and inner masculine selves.

Take a moment to settle yourself here and then call on your feminine self to appear before you. She may appear as a fully clothed woman, or perhaps as a feeling, a shape or a symbol. Trust this energy as an aspect of yourself and when you are ready, ask any questions you may have, such as "Is there anything you would like from me at this time?" or "How can I heal my heart?" Take the time to 'hear' her answers, which may be words, feelings or symbols. Thank your inner feminine for showing up in this way.

Now it is time to invite your masculine self to appear, again asking any questions you may have and trusting in the guidance you receive. Perhaps these two parts of you would like to embrace or communicate their needs to each other, or simply recognise and acknowledge each other. Take your time and when you are ready, thank your masculine self. As you complete the process, return gently from your Heart Temple into present time.

Each time you do this process, you will receive new insights, and perhaps you may want to write them in your journal. Ultimately, when the healing is flowing in your heart chakra, these inner aspects can support each other and come into sacred marriage together.

❖ *Honouring Truthful Communication*

Connecting with, and expressing, the truth and wisdom of your heart, can take courage. Often we try to please others with our responses and this can become a negative pattern of behaviour. Perhaps you grew up in an environment where children were expected to be seen and not heard, and it did not feel safe to speak your truth. Nurturing honesty and integrity in your relationships encourages more trust in truthful communication. When we speak from the heart we open to living our unique truth more fully.

This exercise in self-inquiry can help you to access your own truth and have the courage to clearly express yourself. Take some time to reflect on these questions, perhaps free-writing your responses –

> *"When I am not in my truth – I feel...?"*
> *"What stops me expressing truthfully in my relationships?"*
> *"How does it feel to be totally true to myself?"*
> *"The truth is... (finish the sentence)"*

If you are not used to expressing yourself authentically to others, begin to practice sharing with a trusted friend in a format of 'active listening.' This is where the other person simply listens, without offering advice or feedback. Learn to use the guidance system of your heart to tune in to your feelings first, before responding, when you are asked to do something for others. The saying *"If it's not an absolute* **Yes** *– it's a* **No!***"*, may help you to check in with yourself before agreeing to give out.

❖ Falling in Love with the Healing Power of Nature

Many of us enjoy spending time in nature, perhaps driving through the countryside, sitting or swimming at the beach or walking in the forest. Even in the city it is possible to find a park and sit under a shady tree. How often do we actually open our heart to the healing power of nature and allow ourselves to merge with our surroundings? We usually feel better when we have taken a walk or a swim, yet often our mind is full of thoughts of the 'to do' list or churning over past events. Try this practice of connecting with nature in a different way, just five or ten minutes a day will make a difference.

Sit in your favourite nature spot and imagine you are a tree with roots reaching deeply into Mother Earth. Visualise your base chakra as a beautiful container in which you can sit comfortably. Take a few deep breaths as you settle into your relaxing seat. Invite your spirit to be fully here in this moment. Now bring the awareness to your heart., Breathe into your heart chakra visualising it as a beautiful flower. Notice whether the flower is a new bud or a full bloom – no need to change this, respecting your heart centre is perfect in this moment.

Softly open your eyes and look around you. Choose a tree, plant, flower, stone or animal that you would like to communicate with today. Take in the shape, colour and energy of this, and gently close your eyes again. Form a golden bridge of light between your heart and this beautiful Nature Being; be open to 'hearing' or feeling a message from this amazing aspect of nature. Allow this message to settle in your heart as you give thanks for this moment and your loving earth connection.

Chalice Well, Glastonbury – Historical Facts

The Chalice Well, at the base of Glastonbury Tor, is believed to have sprung from the ground at the site where the 'Holy Chalice' (or the 'Holy Grail') containing drops of the blood of Christ was placed by Joseph of Arimathea. The cover of the Chalice Well is an ancient sacred geometric symbol, the Vesica Pisces, representing the joining of God-Goddess energies. Glastonbury is situated where two powerful ley lines cross in three places, known as the masculine Michael Line and the feminine Mary Line. Standing on these spots can bring a feeling of balance and peace.

Chapter 5

Solar Plexus Chakra

Uluru, Australia

Call of an Ancient Land

In a meditation...

I am lying on the red earth of the Australian desert. I hear water trickling softly into a nearby waterhole; the sound is comforting in the dry heat of the day. For millions of years the Anangu people and the animals have come here to appreciate the water from this source—the only permanent water supply for miles around. I can feel the ancient imprint of these visitors from times gone by, and an inner knowing that I have been here before. I connect with my surroundings and feel myself relaxing into the earth, merging with the warmth of the sand beneath me. The sacred rock towers above me, a guardian of the Dreamtime, a keeper of the dawn of humanity.

My body becomes very still and I am intimately aware of the sounds and smells of the desert, the birds calling and the warm dry air flowing in through my nostrils with the scent of the eucalyptus trees. I feel the rhythm of the earth here–a feeling of softness, a gentle wave-like motion that pulses through the land.

Slipping into another dimension I feel the presence of the Ancestors of this timeless place. The indigenous Grandmothers appear to me one by one, sitting in a circle around me. They gaze upon me with loving eyes, talking softly in their mother-tongue and quietly sharing their thoughts with each other. They are here to perform an initiation ceremony for me. Softly they begin to sing to me, clicking their clap sticks in rhythm. I do not understand the words, yet their chanting washes over me like a soothing balm. My naked body sinks deeper still into the cradle of Mother Earth. The Grandmothers tell me to turn over and lie face down with my belly connected to the earth; an invisible umbilical cord reaches from my navel down into the heart of the Mother. I feel her heartbeat vibrating in my womb and resonating through my body as I lie in the red dirt, being deeply nourished by the Great Mother.

I rest here for some time, until I become aware of an eagle presence within the very centre of the earth. The eagle walks around in a circle, waiting to be released. I feel the vibrant strength of the bird stirring in me as I lie completely still. The Grandmothers indicate I must set the eagle free as a symbol of my own freedom. I slowly sit up and feel the wings of an eagle beginning to form from my shoulders; they begin to gently unfurl, waiting until the time is right for me to fly.

The Grandmothers then guide me to the healing waters of Mutitjulu, where the continual flow of condensation from the rock creates a sacred pool. They gently bathe me, washing the red dirt from my body, cleansing, healing and soothing my soul. When I emerge they walk with me to the sacred rock where I stand with my palms resting against it. I feel the fire energy of the rock warm in my hands and experience the warmth within me beginning to radiate from my solar plexus chakra. My connection with the rock allows me to communicate with the mysteries of the land. The initiation is complete. The Grandmothers bless me with an ochre thumb print symbol on my forehead before dissolving back into the Dreamtime.

Message from Uluru

My first thoughts of Australia came when my friends, Bruce and Janette, decided to move to Adelaide. Bruce was Australian, of Scottish heritage, and they made the trip back to his homeland in 1982 with the invitation for me to visit for a holiday the following year. My love of travel and the opportunity to experience a country so far away was exciting, so I booked my flights to leave England on Boxing Day December 1982.

I flew from the frosty British winter to the 32°C (90°F) heat and the scorched brown hills of Adelaide. It was an enormous culture shock! Bruce and Janette lived in the small town of Strathalbyn, which had a couple of shops, a post office and a pub. One evening Bruce invited me down to the pub for a pre-barbeque drink, I was unprepared to be the only woman in the place apart from the barmaid, as in those days it was typical for only men to frequent the bar. At home in England, in the world of marketing, I was used to entertaining both male and female clients, where it was common for me to not only order the drinks but also pick up the bill. Here in Australia, I was even nervous to approach the bar, but thankfully Bruce made sure I was looked after and soon we went home to Janette who was preparing dinner.

The Australian women I did meet during my stay in Adelaide were strong, forthright and often very opinionated. I found this quite confronting to my polite English upbringing. I later realised the women must have had to generate new resources of inner strength to cope with the conditions of living on the land, and within the strongly male-dominated culture. In fact, a few years later when I moved to Sydney in a senior advertising role, I was shocked at the chauvinistic attitude of many of the men I encountered in the business world.

During my month-long stay, Bruce, Janette and I travelled to the Grampians, a stunning mountain range between Adelaide and Melbourne. We camped in the bush and I had my first experience of kangaroos in the wild. They were not only the cute 'Skippy' type kangaroos I had seen on television, but also huge males who would appear to be standing up on their tails to play violent 'boxing matches', claiming their territory and their right to the females.

We walked for hours in the heat through bush land, listening to the cockatoos squawking, the ear-piercing cicadas and enjoying the potent smell of the eucalyptus trees. At the top of a rocky peak, I looked out across the green forest stretching to the horizon, contrasted against the intense blue of the clear sky as far as my eyes could see. There were no houses or people in sight; this gave me an enormous sense of freedom as I reflected on the English landscape where it was unusual to have wide uninterrupted views. This feeling of freedom and connection with nature had me shedding some clothes and walking top-less through the bush, enjoying the warmth of the sun against my skin, until out of the blue we came upon a family enjoying a picnic beside a waterfall. This made me quickly backtrack to cover myself again, before we greeted each other. The remoteness of this expansive country meant that this family were the only people we met on our long walk and it was a far cry from the

European crowds.

Before coming to Australia, I had considered visiting Uluru, which at the time was commonly known as Ayers Rock, a name given to it by European settlers in 1873 after Sir Henry Ayers, a premier of South Australia. I had seen pictures of the rock in travel brochures offering guided trips and the opportunity to climb it. This appealed to me, so I began to investigate travel options from Adelaide. I had considered traveling on the Ghan train, regarded as one of the world's greatest rail journeys, only to discover that a rare event of heavy rainfall and flooding was taking place in the Red Centre and all trains and buses had stopped running until further notice.

Fortunately, one of the last flights before the floods subsided was about to leave for Alice Springs, I showed up at the airport just in time and got a stand-by ticket. There was not yet an airport at Uluru so access to the Rock was via Alice.

As I boarded the plane, with my glowing suntan and wearing yellow shorts with a skimpy top, an American businessman started chatting me up. During the flight he invited me for dinner at the Alice Springs Casino. I recalled the up-market casinos I had visited in Europe, most requiring membership and strict dress codes. Well, I was in for another massive culture shock. But first there was my meeting with the famous Australian cockroach.

I checked into my motel and noticed an indescribably ugly creature, like nothing I had ever seen before, moving quickly across the wall. It was black and about two inches long and went into a corner where I could no longer see it. The thought of later trying to sleep with it in my room was terrifying, and on entering the bathroom I saw it had a couple of friends there, too. I tried to ignore them, but later that night discovered several of them inside the drawers of the dressing table. I ran to reception but it was already closed, so I waited until the next car drove in and waved it down to help me with the invasion in my room. The lovely Australian couple must have thought I was ridiculous, but nevertheless, the man came and emptied the insect-infested drawers out onto the grass in front of my room and killed a couple more so I could sleep in peace. He reassured me they would not hurt me, "they're just cockroaches, Love", but the thought of them crawling over me in the night was enough to freak me out!

The dinner at the Casino was eye-opening to say the least. The dress code instructed: '*You must wear a shirt, no hats to be worn at betting tables or pokey machines and no thongs (flip flops) allowed.*' This was no problem for me of course, I was dolled up in a pretty dress and heels. I was blown away by the enormous room of slot machines, with flashing lights offering generous and enticing jackpots. The patrons sat in a trance-like stupor with their buckets of coins constantly feeding the machine for hours on end in the hope of a win.

The American man was keen to find a wife to take back home with him and over dinner he shared stories of his traveling lifestyle and the joys of living in the States. Whilst he was a nice guy, and the travel appealed to me, there was no attraction there for me, so we parted ways.

The next morning, for the eight-hour ride out to the Rock, I joined a small group tour to Uluru with eight others, from all over the world. This was before the Lasseter Highway, connecting Alice Springs to Uluru, was fully constructed, so the driver had to navigate the unsealed, red dirt road, skilfully avoiding potholes and crossing over causeways.

The spectacular desert beauty was enhanced by brightly coloured wildflowers in abundance due to the recent rains. Again, the expansive horizon took my breath away. This time it was the rich red colour of the earth contrasted against the intense blue of the sky. At first glimpse, the Rock appeared to emerge from the desert out of nowhere. As we got closer, the sheer size of this huge red monolith, and its stunning grandeur, again took my breath away.

The traditional Aboriginal custodians of Uluru are collectively called Anangu and are made up of three main groups: Pitjantjatjara, Yankunytjatjara and Ngaanyatjara. Uluru is of immense spiritual significance to the Anangu. Their culture indicates that Uluru was formed by Ancestral Beings (Tjukuritja) in the Dreamtime and they believe they are direct descendants of these Beings. The red sandstone rock's many caves and fissures are thought to be evidence of this, with some of the rock forms representing Ancestral Spirits. Today indigenous rituals are still held in the caves around the base of the rock, where many sites are located, sacred to both men and women, and cultural history is passed on to youth through songs.

Our group visits one of these sacred sites, the Mutitjulu

Waterhole, reached by walking along a huge crevice in the base of the rock. I am mesmerised by the water flowing down the side of the rock into the pool, extra deep at this time from the rain. The glistening water flow creates patterns on the rock face that look very feminine. It reminded me of the symbol of the yoni (vagina) in the Hindu tradition, which represents the Shakti, or feminine energy.

Our guide, Peter, tells us traditional stories from the area, shared with him by the indigenous locals. I leave the group to sit on a warm rock and relax and connect with the vibration of this potent place. I imagine the Aboriginal people, especially the women, coming here to collect water along with the animals of the land drinking from the pool for millions of years. I feel the ancient memory of the rock; its energy seems to flow in waves through my body with a welcoming softness. I drop into a deep sleep-like healing meditation, only to be awoken by Peter calling us back to the bus.

Our accommodation, at the foot of Uluru, is an old lodge-style motel with a nearby camp ground inside the national park. This accommodation was closed late in 1983 when construction of the new Yulara Resort was completed and all accommodation was then moved outside the entrance to the park. As the lively group of travellers are bonding over dinner, I chat with Peter and he invites me to see the rock in the moonlight, so we leave the others with their beer and head back to the rock. I had no idea the next couple of hours would completely change the course of my life direction.

Peter was a typical Australian bushman. He had grown up in the great outback and knew the land around Uluru like the back of his hand. He had connections with the local Aboriginal people and had gained some knowledge of their cultural traditions and stories. Most of all he respected the land and the significance of this sacred site, he knew how to be still and listen to the earth. I feel safe and protected with him as we walk back towards Mutitjulu.

The bright light of the full moon illuminates the path as we make our way to the waterhole, with the sounds of the night resonating around us. The cicadas and insects are droning, and even the rock itself seems to emanate a low humming sound as it cools down from the daytime heat. I stop to take in this magnificent moonlit scene and Peter sits quietly nearby enjoying the night air.

As I stand gazing up at the sacred rock, the luminous full moon appears to be balancing on its edge; I feel a shiver go through my body and a deep knowing within every cell of my being that I have to live in this ancient land. I have no idea how this could happen, yet it seems completely right and true in this moment. Here in the moon shadow of the rock, the vibration of trust is so strong. I feel completely supported by the Spirits of the land.

The magic of Uluru was already working on me in potent ways to manifest personal truth and empowerment, and this message resonated deeply with my soul. Looking back, I knew if my life path was to change in such a pivotal way, it would be easy to let go of trying to control the *how* and surrender to the process of *being*.

I now understand the way in which my light body was changed by my time at Uluru. I was receiving what is called an 'energy upgrade'. Put simply, if the vibration of a sacred site is higher than our current energetic vibration, spending time there offers the chance for our auric field to be cleansed and recalibrated to match the vibration of the site. This, in turn, can create profound change and transformation in our life.

The following morning at sunrise, we prepare to climb the rock. The climb is steep and in parts we need to cling to a metal rope chain as we ascend. The rock's plateau is an amazing red sandstone platform, quite flat but with many different crevices and craters. I wander away from the group to take in the stunning view across the desert; my gaze takes in Kata-Tjuta (The Olgas) and travels on to the horizon. The serenity of the sunrise with its soft palette of orange, lilac and pink tones against the sky turning brighter blue by the moment, is a scene like heaven meeting earth. Again I am entranced by the vastness of this country and its breath-taking landscapes.

Back then there was little information provided to visitors about the spiritual and sacred significance of the rock to the Anangu. The land was yet to be handed back to its traditional owners. This happened two years, later in 1985, in a landmark ceremony when the Australian Government handed ownership of this cultural site back to the Aboriginal people. They, in turn, leased the land back to the Commonwealth, for a period of 99 years, so that it could continue to be a site of mutually-managed tourism. Now, years later, as I write about climbing the rock, I feel regretful that I had no idea the local Aboriginal culture believed climbing the rock should only be undertaken by certain initiated men.

The next time I visited Uluru, in the early 1990s, there was more information given to visitors on how to respect the traditional culture of the Anangu—in particular by not climbing the rock. This was clearly stated on the entry pass to the park and on large signs informing visitors "Uluru is sacred in our culture, a place of great knowledge. Please do NOT climb the rock." However, on my last visit in 2010, I was surprised to still see many coach loads of mostly overseas visitors continue to do the climb each day. I would like to believe that if there was more education through tour companies, this activity could be removed from travel itineraries in the future.

Over the next few days, we spent more time exploring the park and visiting the nearby site of Kata-Tjuta, made up of a group of thirty-six rock domes sitting like ancient guardians of the land and dating back 500 million years. This is another culturally sensitive place that traditionally relates to knowledge considered only suitable for initiated men. Interestingly, on the three occasions I have spent time in the Red Centre, I have never felt at home at Kata-Tjuta, it is always Uluru that calls my soul back.

By the time we returned to Alice Springs, I was convinced my move to Australia would happen very soon. This time I chose to stay in the lodge owned by the tour company, avoiding the cockroach-infested motel. The owner was very friendly and suggested he could give me a job driving coach tours out to the rock. I took this as a sign of affirmation and smiled to myself, imagining my advertising colleagues surprise if I were to take him up on his job offer!

Instead. I floated in the above-ground pool under the hot sun and made a clear intention for myself: *If I still feel the same way in one year, I will make plans to move to Australia.*

Love is in the Rock

The next time I experienced the magic of Uluru was nearly ten years later, a few years after I had relocated and become an Australian resident. My sister, Jane, had come to Sydney to visit and we planned a trip together to the Red Centre. My girls were only three and two at the time, so for me to be away for a few days was a big deal, but their dad agreed to care for them and we headed off to the desert.

This time the new Yulara Resort has been built with its own airstrip, so we flew directly to Uluru without going via Alice Springs. We booked accommodation in one of the many options available in the new complex—from ordinary camp sites to 5-star *glamping,* and backpacker rooms to luxury hotels. Renting a car so we could take our time exploring, we stocked up on lots of water, as the temperatures were soaring in January.

As we drove through the park entrance towards the rock, it is getting close to sunset and most visitors are gathering at *sunset strip,* a viewing point where you can observe the distinct colour change in the rock as it reflects the vivid palette of the setting sun—turning red, then deep orange and finally shades of purple. Jane and I choose to avoid the crowds and park up closer to the rock where we enjoy a walk, and then return to relax on the bonnet of the car as dusk falls.

We are captivated by our surroundings as twilight descends on Uluru. The sky changes into soft pinks and subtle violets, and we see shooting stars appearing to fall onto its plateau. The sounds of nature are intense, including the insects making their evening call, and again I hear the now familiar humming vibration of the rock cooling down.

We know the rules of the park are not to sleep or camp close to the rock, but we are mesmerised and lose all track of time as the sky turns to deep indigo blue. Suddenly headlights appear coming towards us, Jane is worried as no one else is around, but I have a feeling it could be the ranger doing his evening rounds. Sure enough he pulls up next to us and asks "Doing a bit of star-gazing girls?" We breathe a sigh of relief and have a friendly chat with him. "Not planning on sleeping out here are you?" he asks, and we reassure him we will head back to the Yulara complex soon.

As he gets back in his vehicle, I ask a last question "Any idea where the moon will rise tonight?" He points over to the horizon where the full moon is rising, a radiant orange ball of light, behind the silhouette of an old coolibah tree. This image is imprinted on my memory forever, as is my previous life-changing encounter with the full moon at Uluru.

The next morning we are up early to do more walking around the base of the rock. We find ourselves drawn back to Mutitjulu waterhole, where we take in the extraordinary shapes that appear to be carved into the rock face above us. One of these is a heart shape.

I point it out to Jane and she agrees, saying, "Inside the heart is the face of my future husband". I look closer and see the face of a man etched into the heart. The face looks just like my friend Bruce at a time when he had a goatee beard. Just as Jane is having the same thought, I say "It looks like Bruce!" The events that unfolded next were clearly Uluru working its manifestation magic again.

Jane already knew Bruce from our friendship in England. In fact at my wedding, Jane was bridesmaid and Bruce was the best man. Now, a few years later, she was single and he was recently divorced. When we returned to Sydney, the two of them reconnected and within a few weeks Bruce had followed Jane back to England. The rest, as they say, is history. Jane and Bruce have now been married for over 20 years and still live on the Northern Beaches of Sydney with my two beautiful nieces.

Return to the Heart of Australia

My connection with Mother Earth, and the predicted planetary changes of 2012, gave me the understanding that the time leading up then would be a time of transformation on many levels. Most significantly, the indications were that many of the controlling patriarchal ways operating in the world would break down as the pendulum swung back after 6,000 years of patriarchy. Ultimately this would create more balance, and a new wave of feminine energy would resurface across the planet.

For energy healers and earth keepers, this new vibration had been anticipated for several years and I had been feeling these energy shifts myself, and observing them in my clients. These powerful changes would require us to be more grounded and balanced in our light body, especially in the heart chakra. One of the ways to sit more comfortably in the heart centre is to release issues of control in the solar plexus chakra. Uluru is the solar plexus chakra of the planet and the heart of Australia, so it felt like perfect timing to finally return in 2010 to create the vibrational essence that could support us during these changes.

The rock had been calling me back again. I had been dreaming about it and feeling the personal significance of its powerful healing energy. This time, the trip would be with four women, friends and earth keepers, together representing the four directions, earth, air, fire and water. Mary had grown up on a farm in rural Australia but had never been out to the Red Centre. Robin, a beautiful sensitive soul, also grew up in Australia and Janie, was a gorgeous earthy Maori woman from New Zealand. At the last minute a younger friend, Chris, decided to join us bringing his supportive male energy to the group.

We flew from Sydney directly to Uluru. The sky was clear and we were blown away by the rare views of Kati Thanda/Lake Eyre full of water from recent floods. This only happens a few times each century, and when it does, it becomes the largest lake in Australia, covering 9,500 square kilometres. The lake is abundant with birdlife and is sometimes called an inland sea, as it sits at 15 metres below sea level and has the same salinity level as the sea.

There are several tributaries flowing into the lake and, from the air, one of these forms the distinct shape of the wetland Brolga bird, the Australian crane, with its large beak, long slender neck and stilt like legs. An Aboriginal Dreamtime story tells of a beautiful girl called Brolga, who was the best and most graceful dancer in the whole land. She liked to make up dances about the wind, the animals and the birds. One day Brolga was taken by an evil Spirit on a gust of wind. When her family went searching for her, the Spirit decided no-one else should have her, and instead turned her into a bird. The Brolga bird may be viewed as a symbol of the sun, the giver of life; it assists us to recharge ourselves on spiritual, emotional and physical levels. With this renewal in our energy, we can then share with others in a more confident, loving and creative way. This message resonates as we make our journey towards the solar plexus chakra of the earth and the personal chakra of the fire within, self-confidence and empowerment.

We are excited when the plane lands and we pick up our car, making it easy for us to go at our own pace and enjoy the park at our leisure. I am the only one in the group who has been here before, and even though I have tried to describe the essence of the place, the powerful yet gentle life force here is a new experience for the others. Immediately on entering the Uluru-Kata-Tjuta National Park, there is a feeling of soft waves of energy permeating through the land. This softness is a strong contrast to the harshness of the sun and dryness of the ground. The healing vibration is present all around, and there is no doubt about the significance of this place as one of the earth's major sacred sites.

Before our trip to the rock, during a healing session, I had this vision relating to the solar plexus chakra which means 'inner sun':

> *I am Fire Woman; I take a stick from the fire and with the indigenous Grandmothers enter a sacred cave within Uluru. As we come into a circle, I light the fire in the middle of the cave. We are in the womb of Uluru and have come to listen to the heartbeat of Mother Earth. As we lie close together with our ears to the ground, I can also hear the sound of the didgeridoo deep within her core. After some time, we sit up, joining hands in a circle as we face the fire to acknowledge our individual fire within.*

I am keen to show the others my favourite place, Mutitjulu Waterhole, so this is where we begin our time at Uluru. We walk along the path, and I notice there is a rope fence running along the base of the rock; this takes me by surprise as there were no fences here on my last visit. As we get closer to the water I see there is also a new metal viewing platform in front of the sacred pool. It is over ten years since my last visit, when the edge of the pool was simply the sandy earth beneath my feet.

At first I feel angry at being kept away from a closer connection with the water, then I realise the platform is probably there to protect the sacredness of the pool. The thing that disturbs me more is the rope fence. A wave of grief arises at the thought of not being able to touch the rock. This grief is not logical, but comes from deep within. My body is yearning to rest against the rock and to feel the warmth and unconditional support. I feel completely distraught at the prospect of not being able to experience this intimate physical connection in the place I love so much.

Fortunately, as we continue our walk around the base of the rock the fence comes to an end, perhaps it is only at the high traffic areas. I immediately collapse against the rock feeling tears of relief welling up inside. I fall into the soft embrace of this sacred place, the familiar feeling of coming home washes over me, as every cell in my body relaxes.

At the pool, there is also a new timber bench made from tree branches so we sit down to enjoy the tranquil scene and to meditate. We all appreciate the sensitivity of our connection with nature, so we stay for a couple of hours in gentle contemplation, tuning into the stillness and the spirits of the water. Every now and again the breeze increases, the water begins to ripple, and shortly afterwards a new group of people arrive to visit the pool. Most of them are with a tour guide, making a lot of noise and quickly taking as many photos as possible before continuing on their way.

As the group leaves, the breeze dies down and the water becomes still again. We quietly observe as this happens over and over again. It appears the nature spirits are aware each time new energy enters the space. We have subtly merged with our surroundings, even though we have only been here a short time, and we feel a little sad for the visitors who are not given the time to sit in stillness during their time in this magical spot.

We finally return to our accommodation, where it is buzzing with visitors from all around the world, particularly European guests, as it is summer holiday time over there. It is a quite overwhelming coming from our meditative state into the huge bar and eating area, where cooking your own meat on the barbie is the order of the day—a bit of a challenge for the vegetarians among us! Then it is time for an early night, ready to enjoy sunrise the next morning and complete our mission to create the essence.

At daybreak, the rising sun reflected on the rock is a stunning spectacle of colour. Sadly the scene at the viewing area is disappointing, where hoards of visitors are loudly talking in many languages. These organised areas are all new to me, and I wish to find a quieter place where we can drop into more serenity again.

The Uluru–Kata-Tjuta National Park Knowledge Handbook requests visitors to observe the three R's:

> **Relationship** - *recognise Indigenous people's relation-ship and connection to the land.*
> **Responsibility** - *acknowledge the on-going responsibility Indigenous people have to country and recognise your own responsibility of travelling thoughtfully.*
> **Respect** - *respect Aboriginal beliefs associated with country and culture.*

I am curious to know if loud talking and shouting at sunrise could be seen as not travelling thoughtfully?

We decide to make the ten kilometre walk around the base of Uluru, allowing us to feel into the land and choose the perfect location to make the essence. The scenery is spectacular; there are many formations within the rock that resemble creatures and indigenous spirits. One area looks just like a whale with its huge mouth open, another like the tail of a kangaroo and many appear as faces of people carved into the rock face. It is an easy flat walk that takes in many of the sacred sites around the rock. Some of these are female ceremonial sites and some male, all are marked clearly and some ask for cultural respect by not taking photos of the area.

Much of the walk we undertake in silence, as we are all having our own personal experience of being out here in the desert. The native flowering bushes are beautiful, and Janie, who is a homeopath, points out different healing plants and encourages us to smell the exquisite perfume of the native bushes. Janie has made the intention to walk the Indigenous *songlines*, and Uluru sits where some of the major songlines or energy pathways converge. The Aboriginal people also refer to the songlines as *dreaming tracks*, paths across the earth that mark the route followed by the 'creator beings' during the Dreamtime.

Janie wanders off the track, walking barefoot and letting her feet guide her, quietly singing to herself and the land. Suddenly she looks up to see an old male dingo coming directly towards her. Her first thought is that the dingo is an Ancestral Being or a Gatekeeper of Uluru. He looks straight into her eyes as if saying "Hello" and keeps on walking until they step around each other. Janie does not feel afraid; her feeling is more one of being acknowledged by a guardian and protector of the land.

Some of the areas we pass do not feel welcoming, so we keep on walking, other places energetically invite us in to explore further. We savour each new bend and crevice with curiosity, and are completely enchanted by every new scene. Some of the trees look like old Guardians with images of faces appearing on their gnarly trunks, and the whole area is full of Nature Devas and Spirit Beings. To the Anangu, these features are related to the journeys and actions of Ancestral Beings across the landscape.

When we have almost completed our walk, we finally find the spot for making the essence. This is on the east side of the rock, facing towards Kata-Tjuta, in an area where the rock meets the earth with a low slope. We intuitively ask for permission from the Ancestral Guardians of the land, and all feel a resounding 'yes' to our request.

The place we have chosen is not far from Mala Putra, an Anangu women's site and sacred in traditional Tjukuritja law. A visitor sign informs us '...*the rock details and features are equivalent to a sacred scripture and these stories are passed down from Grandmother to Granddaughter in an oral culture. Tjukuritja knowledge is earned and with it comes cultural responsibility'*.

We are appropriately respectful of the cultural sensitivity of this nearby site, as we set up the bowl of pure water resting in a natural hollow in the rock, surrounded by crystals and feathers we have found along the way. We acknowledge and give thanks to the traditional custodians of the land and call on the seven directions for support, with this prayer from Jose Arguelles, a South American teacher who shared his wisdom of the Mayan calendar and the major shift due to occur in 2012:

Prayer to the Seven Directions

From the East, House of Light
May wisdom dawn in us
So we may see all things in clarity.
From the North, House of Night
May wisdom ripen in us
So we may know all from within.
From the West, House of Transformation,
May wisdom be transformed into right action
So we may do what must be done.
From the South, House of the Eternal Sun,
May right action reap the harvest
So we may enjoy the fruits of planetary being.
From Above, House of Heaven,
Where star people and ancestors gather

May their blessings come to us now.
From Below, House of Earth,
May the heartbeat of her crystal core
Bless us with harmonies to end all war.
From the Centre, Galactic Source,
Which is everywhere at once
May everything be known as the light of mutual love.
Oh Yum Hunab Ku Evam Maya E Ma Ho
All Hail the Harmony of Mind and Nature

We then sit in meditation while the water captures the unique vibration of Uluru, the planetary solar plexus chakra. The solar energy is evident by the heat generated by the rock during the day; the solar plexus is a fire centre and the power chakra. The rock was formed over 500 million years ago. The part we can see is the 348-metre-high tip, yet geologists believe it reaches over two kilometres down into the earth, meaning even more of its enormous mass is deeply anchored into Mother Earth.

We all sink into the profound stillness offered by the mother energy in this timeless space where minutes, hours or even days, could pass without noticing. Here in the desert, the overwhelming feeling is one of releasing the need to control ourselves and our lives, to simply enjoy the power of sitting in stillness. As we soften in the solar plexus. it is easier to gently move into our heart chakra without struggle or force. Uluru offers this gift of letting go to experience the present moment and truly experience 'heaven on earth'.

Each of us is profoundly and uniquely touched by our time spent communing with the rock. We feel complete when the Mother Tincture for the essence is ready to be bottled. As always, the essence has been made in divine timing, with grace and the support of the Ancestors. We express our enormous gratitude to Uluru and to all of the seen and unseen Beings who have supported this magical journey.

Respecting the Grandmothers

Following our beautiful time at Uluru, we decide to drive out to Kata-Tjuta. Chris is especially interested in visiting this male initiation site. I am curious to tune into the site again to see if anything has changed for me since my last visit.

One of the most well-known areas of Kata-Tjuta is the Valley of the Winds, and as we pull up in the car park, this is clearly an appropriate name. The wild wind almost bowls us over as we struggle to get out the car. At the beginning of the walk, a visitor sign states

"Kata-Tjuta is sacred to Anangu men. The traditional law for Kata-Tjuta is still learnt and passed on today. Under this Law, detailed knowledge of the area is restricted to certain people only. It is forbidden to pass this information on to the wrong people. Therefore we cannot share any of the creation stories with you. In the old days, Anangu would walk to Kata-Tjuta from lands to the west. The stream flowing out from Walpa Gorge has always been an important source of water. Women would camp well back from the Gorge around the area where the picnic ground now sits."

Reading this confirms my previous feeling of not being welcomed here, so Mary, Robin and I choose to stay out of the wind in the car while Janie and Chris head out towards the Valley of the Winds. However, they go no further than the entrance to the valley, feeling the powerful Spirits around them, and recalling ancient memories of this sacred initiation site.

Later, we visit the new Cultural Centre, where traditionally crafted pu n u (wooden object) tools and artefacts are displayed along with new art forms from Anangu craftspeople of the western desert region. The art gallery is owned and operated by local artists from the Mutitjulu Community and sells paintings, ceramic art, jewellery and other merchandise with local designs.

I am drawn to a vibrant string of colourful beads made by the indigenous Grandmothers. The necklace is crafted from a combination of bright yellow quandong seeds and red/brown ininti seeds. The seeds and the golden colour appeal to me for their connection with the solar plexus chakra.

It is not until I am back at home and working with clients that I experience the true medicine of this ceremonial jewellery. I drape the necklace on an African carving of a pregnant woman in a spot where I can see it while conducting healing sessions. Every now and then, as I am immersed in supporting a client, particularly with issues involving the solar plexus chakra, the necklace will *call* to me. I trust my connection with it and feel compelled to bring it into the healing.

Letting my client know what is happening, I offer to place it around their neck, where it rests over the heart chakra and reaches down to the solar plexus centre. We feel the Spirits of the indigenous Grandmothers entering the room and forming a protective circle around us, offering support and healing. Almost immediately, the energy softens and together we are able to get to the core of the issue easily and gracefully. I am enormously grateful for the powerful medicine the necklace carries, and its connection with Uluru and the Grandmothers. I feel privileged to be its keeper.

Protecting the Sacred Waters

In 2016, as I am writing, there is a significant event occurring in North America. First Nations people from three hundred tribes are gathered at Standing Rock to protect the waters of Lake Oahe, a dammed up portion of the Missouri River system that stretches downstream more than 1,000 miles into the Mississippi River. These sacred waters are under threat from the planned construction of an oil pipeline that could threaten their sole water source and their ceremonial lands.

Sadly, the mainstream media are giving minimal coverage to the violence experienced by the Water Protectors of Standing Rock as the American Government sent in troops. The news comes through social media, from those participating in the peaceful action. A worldwide meditation is held to offer prayers to the Oceti Sakowin Reservation (commonly known as the Sioux) and their tribal lands in North Dakota.

I participate with a local meditation group and we offer our prayers to the water sources of the world. Forming an energetic link through the ley lines to Uluru, we connect with the healing waters of Mutitjulu, and feel our prayers for protection and peace flow through the waterways into the earth. This river of healing light flows to Standing Rock and beyond, in solidarity with the indigenous people as they are holding a prayerful protest on behalf of all sacred waters. The following week, the Obama administration denies the final access for the pipe to cross under Lake Oahe, instead ordering an Environmental Impact Statement to explore alternative routes. This is a small step towards addressing the greed and control of the oil companies, and a recognition of the wisdom carried by the Indigenous Nations.

I have great respect for each of the earth chakras as potent healing portals for planetary healing, yet Uluru continues to have enormous significance in my life. As I write, I am again feeling the call to sit with the sacred rock and I plan to take the finished book with me to the place where the second half of my life began in Australia. I will ask for blessings for the book to be received by its readers as both my personal memoir and as a guide to the healing offered by the sacred sites around the world.

Healing Inspiration from Uluru – Solar Plexus Chakra

❖ ***Sitting in Stillness - Releasing Patterns of Control***
The solar plexus chakra (Manipura) is the centre of personal power, the energy of 'control' also sits here. In this chakra, we can experience both fear (control) or confidence and empowerment. Patterns of control are like a layer of protective clothing that does not allow us to feel our surroundings or to connect within ourselves. When we live or work in a highly stressful environment, staying in control may help us to feel safe and protected. The desire to stay continually in control of our lives and our surroundings is a form of addiction.

There may have been a time in your life when this protection was appropriate, perhaps as a child when you needed to feel safe from difficult situations or abuse, rarely letting your guard down to experience or express your feelings. The protection may no longer serve you. Taking time to reconnect with your inner self can bring more acceptance, confidence and joy.

MEDITATION
Sitting in a quiet place, perhaps in nature, create your grounding connection to Mother Earth, like the roots of a tree. Bring your awareness to the solar plexus chakra, between the navel and the heart. Imagine there is a warm and safe cave inside your chakra, gently approach the opening to the cave and when you are ready enter the doorway to this sacred space within. You may wish to invite a spirit guide, guardian angel or totem animal to join you. In the centre of the cave is a small fire burning softly, illuminating the walls. Take the time to look around and slowly explore the cave. How does it feel? Allow yourself to come closer to the warming fire.

Now invite an aspect of yourself who has felt controlled or the need to be guarded (protected) to join you by the fire. This may be a younger aspect of yourself (your inner child) or an aspect that has felt controlled at any stage of your life.

As you sit together, imagine the warmth from the fire drawing out and releasing any fears or rigidity you have been carrying within. Connect with your breath to release these qualities on the exhalation. Think of a time in your life when you have felt safe and protected, begin to connect with the energies of security and empowerment, breathe these in on the inhalation.

Take the time to relax within yourself, ask for guidance and support from the spirits of the cave within. Using your breath to relax, let yourself drop into deep stillness, feeling the potential for peace within. Whenever you feel ready to leave this sacred space, ensure you bring any symbolic tools with you into daily life.

When you finish the meditation, check in with yourself and feel what kind of protection is most appropriate in your life today. This could be a protective bubble, a flower or a symbol, imagine this at the edge of your aura giving you room to breathe and to experience your own light shining from within.

❖ Respecting Indigenous Cultures and the Sacred Sites

The indigenous peoples of the world have great respect for their sacred sites. In many different cultures, offerings are made to the mountain, the sacred waters, the trees, plants and elemental kingdom. When we visit a sacred site, it is worthwhile gaining an understanding of how the local people acknowledge or celebrate the place as one of spiritual significance.

The earth chakras are connected through the ley lines deep within the earth. This means that when we journey from one side of the world to the other, we carry a little of the energy of our homelands with us. We can be more respectful of this by taking the time to ground and centre ourselves before we enter new places. It is important to ask the spirits of the land for permission and to have regard for notices or signs relating to the local practices.

Follow your heart when you hear the call from a particular sacred site. If you are not able to visit physically, connect with it from afar, tune into the spirits of the land and see if they have a message or request for you. Trust your intuition to guide you appropriately and offer healing to the land. Mother Nature is a wonderful healer. When we take time to sit in stillness, with her arms around us, magic happens.

❖ Appreciating the Unconditional Love of the Elders, Earth Keepers & Spiritual Teachers

Throughout the world the Indigenous Elders respect the earth. The Grandmothers, Grandfathers, Earth Guardians and Spiritual Teachers are in constant heart connection with Mother Earth. They feel the planetary changes on a cellular level and hold the wellbeing of our home on earth in their hearts. Growing up in a Western civilisation, we have not always been taught or shown role models of this way of respect, honouring our ancestors or living on the land, as people of the land.

Aboriginal Elder and one of the Traditional Custodians of Uluru (Ayers Rock), Uncle Bob Randall, a 'Tjilpi (special teaching uncle), shared a powerful message of *Kanyini*, the interconnectedness of every living thing being not just an idea but a way of life. He explains that all beings are part of a vast family and calls us to be responsible for this family and to care for the land with unconditional love and responsibility. We have much to learn from this message shared by many native and spiritual teachers around the world. [6]

Another message of interconnectedness comes from the Dalai Lama:

"If we want a beautiful garden, we must first have a blueprint in the imagination—a vision. Then that idea can be implemented and the external garden can materialize. Destruction of nature resources results from ignorance, lack of respect for the Earth's living things, and greed. In the first place we must strive to overcome these states of mind by developing an awareness of the interdependent nature of all

phenomena, an attitude of wishing not to harm other living creatures and an understanding of the need for compassion." The Ten Eternal Questions 7

Uluru, Australia – Historical Facts

Uluru is a massive sandstone monolith in the heart of the central Australian desert. It is 450km from the nearest large town, Alice Springs. A significant sacred site for indigenous Australians, and believed to be about 500 million years old. The Aboriginal people, the *Anangu,* believe the Central Australian landscape was created at the beginning of time, known as the 'Dreamtime', by ancestral beings.

Chapter 6

Sacral Chakra

Lake Titicaca, Bolivia & Peru

Entering the Womb of Mother Earth

I have a vision...

I enter the Temple of my Womb, the inner sanctuary of my sacral chakra. The space is glowing with amber light, and inside my sensual self is dancing. Soft veils in warm colours of orange, red and golden fabric move gently around my naked body. I feel the freedom of my movements as I dance in celebration of the divine feminine within. The sound and vibration of music flows through me as I embody this exquisite part of myself.

In the centre of the temple a golden flame burns brightly and I notice a separate Priestess aspect of myself. She is dressed in white and is kneeling in devotion to the flame, a symbol of the sacred feminine. My Priestess self is following a path of devotion; she is in Universal service to humanity, to help reclaim and heal the wounds of the feminine. During this time of realising greater balance between female and male energies on the planet, a profound healing energy has flowed through me in my work and in my personal life. I have received the light of the flame for self-healing and have shared it with others on the path of reclaiming the sacred feminine. I now see it is time to set my devotional self free and allow her to move into a time of celebrating more sensuality in daily life.

My sensual self moves towards my devotional self and invites her to dance. Slowly these two aspects come to face each other; they embrace and gently begin to move together. Warm passionate colours blend into the aura of the devotional self, creating a feeling of tenderness and flow as they merge to dance as one in celebration of life and the safe expression of the sacred feminine.

The Gift of Receiving

In the lead up to the year 2012, ancient prophesies from many indigenous traditions, including the Mayan, Incan, Hopi and Vedic traditions, came to light. The records of the Mayan Timekeepers showed that 2012 would mark the close of several great cycles of time: a 26,000 year Mayan calendar cycle, a 78,000 year Earth cycle, a 26 million year Earth cycle and a 225 million Galactic Year. The simultaneous close of these cycles was likened to the odometer turning over for the entire history of our galaxy, and perhaps the whole cosmos. This would be a moment when humanity was expected to take a huge leap in evolution on all levels.

Spiritual teachers spoke of a shift in the balance of patriarchal and matriarchal relating—a time when women would again have the opportunity to offer spiritual leadership from the feminine perspective. With this redress of male-female balance, we would see more female leaders in the business world, religious organisations and governments, with more opportunities for women to light the way forward in a harmonious way.

My own insights revealed past-life memories of the ancient civilisation of Atlantis, a sophisticated culture that began with a foundation of equilibrium, gender equality, highly attuned psychic awareness and the skills to work with the healing power of crystals. I recall memories where I lived a life of balance and joy in the Temples of Atlantis, living in harmony with my soul family, including our dolphin brothers and sisters.

There were also memories of other more challenging times, when the patriarchal power was used in abusive ways and the matriarchal lineage was controlled and oppressed. Some legends say Atlantis was a utopia destroyed by an earthquake; other beliefs say the misuse of crystal technology, to gain power and control, ultimately created the fall of this advanced civilisation.

In the years leading up to 2012, much of my own healing focus had been on bringing my masculine and feminine aspects into balance. The recurring message was to heal all the past wounds of

Atlantis in order to restore my soul's original blueprint and come back into right relationship with myself, in my connections with others and with Mother Earth.

When I separated from my husband, and moved away from Sydney, one of my clear intentions was to create a stable home for myself and my daughters. I also had a long-time vision to set up a healing centre where people could come to rest and replenish. Fortunately, I was able to draw on investments from my previous career and purchase a beautiful property in the Byron Bay hinterland. The divine nature around the property included a paddock for the girls' horses, a pocket of mature rainforest trees next to a river and a hidden glade filled with fairies and elemental devas.

I named the property Tranquil Sanctuary, and it was truly a sanctuary and retreat from the day-to-day world. Many friends, clients and students were uplifted by simply entering the magical garden. It was also an idyllic place for the girls to thrive through their teenage years, enjoying the space to ride their horses, play with the dogs and hang out with their friends. The property nurtured our family for ten years, during which time we created a Medicine Wheel (Native American healing circle), conducted regular Hindu Havan rituals (sacred fire pujas for planetary healing), held pregnancy retreats and ran workshops and trainings in spiritual healing.

In the years leading up to 2012, I began to find it more and more difficult to meet the mortgage payments. Interest rates were high and my work as a Childbirth Educator and Spiritual Healer did not yield a regular nine-to-five routine, or a fixed income stream. I knew this was a choice I made when I left the high-paying world of marketing, yet the negative conditioning I grew up with, of having to work hard to make a living, began to rear its ugly head and doubts arose about how following my soul path could support staying at the property.

My greatest wish was to provide a secure home until both my daughters had finished school. Every month I became increasingly stressed and distraught about making the payments to the bank, yet my heart was telling me to stay in the home we loved. At first I tried to do the English thing of 'stiff upper lip' and not share my distress with anyone. Then one day, I let down my guard and shared my vulnerability with a friend, and unexpectedly a magical thing happened ... "I'd like to help you, I can lend you the mortgage payment," she offered. At first I looked at her in disbelief, and then tears of relief started streaming down my face. I felt my heart open to receive her gift of loving kindness.

This act of generosity initiated a stream of support, which came pouring in from friends and family over the next months, enabling us to stay there until the girls left home. For me this support was a clear acknowledgment of following my soul path. Even more significantly, I was able to release one of my core patterns of always being the strong one supporting others. By showing my vulnerability, I opened the way to receive unconditional love and support instead.

Initially the encouragement came from my female friends, women who felt the importance of keeping the family home; then later, from male friends who also trusted and believed in me. I have so much gratitude for those who supported me through this difficult time. It was a huge process of transformation to let go of past restrictive beliefs and to trust in continuing the work that truly makes my heart sing. The more I align myself with my soul path, the easier it is to accept the synchronistic flow of universal support.

I had a light-bulb moment a few years ago when I realised that birth and healing are both natural and organic processes – they always occur with divine timing. On reflection, my business also has its own organic stages of growth, often not following strict budgets and forecasts, its evolution occurs naturally. When I accept this process and use the quiet times to gestate new ideas and nurture my creativity, there is more flow in both my work and my life.

When I reflect on the sacral chakra as the female creative centre, where we conceive, gestate and birth, not only our babies but also our creative ideas, I understand for myself, like many women who are the sole or primary parent of their children, that one of the on-going challenges is to maintain balance in this chakra rather than giving out more than we receive. As a woman, I know it is possible to 'have it all,' yet I can still get caught up in the patriarchal paradigm of stress and over-achieving, trying to juggle many balls to fit into a false belief system.

When I take the time to celebrate the fact that 'I am enough' in each of my roles, especially in my responsibility as a mother, I feel more fulfilled. I also love to acknowledge other mothers in the valuable and worthy role of mothering, from the birth of babies to the sometimes-challenging time of the teenage years. I refer to my own *mothering career* as one of my greatest achievements in raising soulful and aware young women who know the value of true connection.

The Pilgrim's Way

On New Year's Eve, 2011, I was gifted a Rebirthing Breathwork session, a conscious, connected body/breath process where pain, memories or feelings can surface to be released, cleared or resolved. This was the perfect way for me to end a stressful year and bring more consciousness into my intentions for the coming months. During the session, I received many visions, including one of lying naked on the grass in the magical garden of my property. The spirits of the land and tree guardians were supporting me to let go and relax, to allow my body to soften and to be held by Mother Earth. I felt a deep sense of peace washing over me and looking down at my bare skin, I saw small green shoots of new growth appearing… a sign of new beginnings.

This vision gave me encouragement in the coming months, although the new growth did not manifest until almost the end of the year. For much of the time, I was in pain, my body was showing physical signs of the stress; my left shoulder had bursitis, a painful inflammation of the fluid that lubricates the joints. I was very aware this was my feminine side needing support as I 'shouldered' much of the responsibility alone.

On the other side of the world, my daughter, Amber, was travelling, with plans for a pilgrimage of her own, to walk *El Camino de Santiago*, (The Way of St. James) across Spain. The walk is also known as the Pilgrim's Way and offers several different pilgrimage routes, including the one beginning in Saint-Jean-Pied-de-Port on the French border and stretching over 750 kilometres to its culmination at the cathedral city of Santiago de Compostela. This was the way Amber chose to walk alone.

The Camino is a spiritual journey, offering a time of contemplation, reflection and the opportunity to meet other pilgrims. In times gone by, it provided a way of 'walking off one's sins', and legend says that the Camino offers the healing each individual needs and that pilgrims may also find love along the way. I was a little anxious, with Amber's decision to walk by herself, yet I understood this was her soul calling and trusted she would be supported.

From the day she started walking, our heart connection was strong and whenever she had an internet connection she would message me with her progress. She found herself walking with a group of men, ranging in age from 23 to 73, each one with their own deeply personal motivation to complete the walk to Santiago. They gave her companionship and caring masculine support as they walked, knowing they were looking out for her, made me less concerned for her safety too.

My heart longed to accompany her. In my meditations, Spanish spirit guides were appearing and at night I was dreaming of walking the path beside her. We had talked about the possibility of me joining her, at least for the last 100 kilometres, but as the time got closer and finances got tighter, I regretfully accepted this would not be possible. We had no idea that we would make a different pilgrimage to one of the earth chakras together later that year. Neither did we know that destiny and love had other divine plans for Amber as she continued the walk.

The group's arrival in Santiago was a joyful celebration; Amber had formed strong connections with each of the men, even though they did not speak the same language. By the end of the walk she had become the 'adopted' granddaughter of Juan, the eldest man, who was walking the Camino after recovering from cancer. Five years later they continue to stay in touch and meet whenever possible.

In Santiago, most of her group had finished their journey but Amber decided to continue on to Finisterre, known as the 'End of the World', where the way meets the Atlantic Ocean and pilgrims can purify their bodies in the sea. It was on this final stretch of the path that Amber met Victor, a friendly, charismatic Spanish guy from Majorca, and they completed the walk together. They agreed to stay in touch as Amber was continuing her travels in Europe and South America. It was not until the following year, when Victor came to Sydney, that their love really blossomed. They have now been together for four years, including a year living back in Spain. As Victor says, for the two of them it really was "The Camino of Love!"

Islands of the Sun and Moon

Towards the end of 2012 I had the opportunity to attend a childbirth conference in San Francisco. At the same time, my longing to travel to Lake Titicaca, on the border of Bolivia and Peru, was still strong after my last attempt had been blocked. I knew that from America, flights to Peru would be cheaper, so saying a prayer to the angels of travel, I set off to California.

Amber was still traveling; she had visited Brazil, Uruguay, Argentina and Bolivia and was making her way to Peru. She had been away for eighteen months, so I was desperate to hug her and as soon as I found a cheap flight we made plans to meet up in Peru. We were coming from different directions and the most convenient place to meet was the small oasis town of Huacachina, famous for its rolling sand dunes, including Cerro Blanco, the highest dune in the world.

I really enjoy the fact that my daughters have both inherited my own love of adventure. I delight in their grounded and street-wise approach to travel, especially when they now direct me on how to get around in foreign countries. Amber's instructions for traveling to meet her went something like this "Ok, Mum, when you arrive in Lima, you get a hostel for the night. Next morning you get up early and walk to the bus station to buy a ticket to Ica on the bus that leaves later in the day. You book the 'cama' seat, which reclines, so you can sleep for some of the five hour trip and I will meet you at the bus station." All very straight forward, but not taking into account the increasing altitude as the bus climbs up progressively winding roads in the darkness, making it impossible for me to sleep or even close my eyes without feeling nauseated.

By the time the bus arrived in Ica, I could not wait a moment longer to squeeze my girl, even the severe altitude sickness could not take away the joy of our emotional reunion. We were both crying and hugging each other tightly in the middle of the bus station. In our hostel room, we stayed awake for hours catching up on Amber's stories of travel and making plans for our own time together and the journey to the sacred lake.

The next morning was surreal awaking at the oasis of

Huacachina, it felt just like we were somewhere in the Middle East, with the exception of camels. The sand dunes are awesome in the true meaning of the word. The tiny town, with a population of about one hundred, is built around a natural lake in the desert and is renowned for sand boarding and dune buggy riding, with thousands of tourists coming to enjoy the sports all year round. This was a part of Peru I had not visited before and it made me more aware of the varied landscapes and scenery of this fascinating country.

I was prepared to suffer some altitude sickness, but this time it hit me pretty hard. The familiar symptoms of breathlessness, exhaustion and nausea took almost a week to disappear. Amber had come from Bolivia and was already acclimatised. We knew there was a full moon eclipse coming up later in the week, and wanted to reach Lake Titicaca to see this, however, I needed to take things slowly. We spent an extra day in the colonial city of Arequipa, which sits at 2,328 metres above sea level and is surrounded by three volcanoes. I again drank the local altitude remedy of coca tea, but also tried an espresso frappuccino, plenty of rest and ice cream, which all seemed to help!

Finally we set off to Puno on the shores of Lake Titicaca, and home to the floating reed Uros islands. The Uros natives call themselves Kotsuna, 'the lake people', and their origins go back to eras before the Incas. The islands are made of totora reeds, which grow in the lake, the dense roots of the plants develop and interweave forming a natural layer, one to two meters thick, that supports the islands. There are more than forty floating islands, with the larger ones being home to up to ten Uros families.

The local people still live a mostly traditional lifestyle, using the reeds not only to build their homes and impressive boats, but also as food and medicine. Although one of the newer initiatives is the recycling of discarded plastic bottles, built into the reed structure of the boats, this helps them to stay afloat longer. Tourists are now welcome and the women warmly invited us into their homes, sharing their way of life and selling indigenous crafts and colourful weaving to supplement their income. There was an opportunity to spend a night on the floating islands, sleeping in a simple reed hut and enjoy the sunrise, but this time we were headed for other islands: the Isla del Sol and the Isla de la Luna.

Our trip involved taking another bus through the Andes

Mountains and across the border into Bolivia to the lakeside town of Copacabana. At the checkpoint we all get off the bus to have our passports stamped and then climbed back on again a few metres down the road. Lake Titicaca is the highest navigable lake in the world at 3,812 metres elevation. It is 8,372 square kilometres in size and straddles the border between Peru and Bolivia. From the shore, it stretches farther than the eye can see, and it is hard to imagine that you are not standing on the seashore.

We spent the night in Copacabana, and arranged to catch the ferry to the Isla del Sol (Island of the Sun) the next morning. The ferry carried us along with a group of local Quechua women and children, all dressed in colourful traditional attire, along with a few backpackers. Amber had already visited the lake on her way from Bolivia and was keen to share her discoveries with me, including a spot she had found on the island where I could perhaps make the essence. I was strongly guided to visit both islands symbolising the balance of the sun/moon and male/female energies. As there was no accommodation on the Isla de la Luna (Island of the Moon) Amber continued on ahead of me to find a place to stay on the Isla del Sol.

I alighted from the ferry on the Isla de la Luna and began to walk up the solitary path with a handful of other visitors. I let them go ahead to enjoy the panoramic vistas, the serenity of the island and take in the silent stillness of the lake. With the exception of a few grazing llamas and sheep, I was now alone.

Settling myself beside an old rock wall to meditate, I began to feel the deep tranquillity of my surroundings. Suddenly I noticed a Quechua woman in her colourful wide skirt, woven shawl and vibrant hat, slowly making her way up the hillside below. This made me feel curious, as I did not notice any of the local women get off the ferry.

> *I close my eyes and begin to tune into the surroundings, taking the time to ground myself by visualising my roots connecting deeply into the island and down into the floor of the lake. I have waited a long time to get to this earth sacral chakra, and I want to make the most of my time here. I wonder if the local woman will mind me sitting here, so I look up to check and she is still climbing the path. Settling myself again, I drop into deep meditation, and almost*

> *immediately a female spirit guide dressed just like the Quechua woman, appears next to me. She welcomes me to the island and offers me a conch shell, from which I must drink the restorative waters of the lake. I feel the water pouring into my mouth and washing down my throat—like a healing elixir. The guide hands me the conch shell as a gift and I thank her.*

This experience only lasted for a short time, yet when I opened my eyes, the woman climbing had completely disappeared. She was no longer below or above me on the path. I continued to walk to the other side of the island to pick up the next ferry and she was still nowhere to be seen. I sent a prayer of gratitude to this spirit guide who has welcomed me and pondered over the idea of drinking the actual water from the lake.

Lake Titicaca is said to be the cradle of Peru's ancient civilisations, with links to numerous Andean cultures, including Aymara (pre-Incan), the Purakas, the Tiwanakus and the Incas who hold it as a sacred site. The Incan creation myth tells of the god Con Tiqui Viracocha emerging from Lake Titicaca, bringing some human beings with him. He commanded the sun (Inti), moon (Mama Quilla) and the stars to rise. Viracocha created more human beings from stone, bringing them to life and commanding them to go and populate the world. The Incas therefore believed Lake Titicaca was their place of origin, and that when they died, their spirits would return to this lake.

Mama Quilla (Mama Kilya), wife of Inti the sun god, is the Moon Mother and the regulator of women's menstrual cycles, as the waxing and waning of the moon was used to calculate monthly cycles. Seasonal festivals and celebrations to honour Pachamama (Earth Mother) were also set by these rhythms. The Pleiades star cluster was known as the 'little mothers', and festivals were celebrated on their reappearance in the sky.

These stories felt ever present as we spent time at the lake. There was an atmosphere of soothing tranquillity and calm peacefulness. It is impossible to ignore the effects of all the elements being here on top of the world, surrounded by the vast blue waters and expansive clear blue skies, breathing in the fresh quality of the air and getting lost in the galaxies stretching to infinity at night-time.

Amber was waiting for me at the Isla del Sol. She took my bag as I struggled with the breath-taking climb up more than 200 steps, a path built by the Incas, to the village of Yumani where we would stay the night. Our accommodation is a simple room with a view of the lake, costing just forty Bolivianos (approximately seven dollars) a night. Luckily there was very little to buy on the island, as there are no banks and we have made a mistake calculating our Bolivian currency. Amber reassured me she had plenty of bolivianos left over, and I only had Peruvian sol but later she realised her mistake and that we are short of cash, and no-one accepts payment by card.

We laughed as we stretched our budget buying meals to share and enjoying the local quinoa soup together. The exquisite location more than made up for the enforced diet. There is a beautiful simplicity of life on the island and we found ourselves dropping easily into this rhythm. We climbed to the highest point where there is a small Inca temple and views across the lake to the Isla de la Luna. Amber was right, this was the perfect place for the essence, and I set it up on the earth below the temple, protected by shrubs, as it would stay here overnight to be infused with the light of the lunar eclipse.

At sunset, we slowly descended from the temple, passing several locals making their way home up the path, some women with a baby cosily strapped to their back and others encouraging their donkeys to get a move on. They called out cheerful greetings and one grandmother even stopped to get her breath "It's hard, I am tired" she said as we passed, perhaps I am not the only one feeling the altitude.

We stopped to watch the full pink moon rising over the lake, casting a shimmering path across the waters, and I felt overcome by the divine beauty of this moment, standing there with my daughter, surrounded by Mother Nature in all her magnificence. The previous stresses and struggles of the months before just melted away as we stood transfixed by the sight of the moon reflected on the water.

A lunar eclipse occurs when the moon and the sun are directly aligned with the earth in the middle; the moon then passes directly behind the earth into its shadow. The time of an eclipse often creates heightened emotions and gives the opportunity to discover our true feelings. Here at the sacral (emotional) chakra of the world, this intense astrological influence, coupled with the creative forces of nature, is truly a gift of release and transformation for me.

The next day we continued to explore the island, and Amber gave herself a purifying initiation by taking a squealing dip in the freezing waters of the lake, while I followed the guidance of my spirit guide by drinking a little of the waters, as if taking a homeopathic remedy. The essence was completed and bottled, capturing the unique vibration of Lake Titicaca and the potency of the lunar eclipse in the mother tincture for others to experience. The now familiar feeling of contentment washed over me as another of the earth chakra pilgrimages had been fulfilled.

Amaru Muru - Stargate Doorway

I know my time with Amber would be short, but I was unprepared when it came time to separate again. We boarded the bus back to Puno where I would spend the night and Amber was to take a night bus to Chile. The bus was full and there were no seats for us together. Unexpectedly, I began to cry, feeling my sadness at parting again. Amber comforted me and a single English woman invited me to sit with her. She was friendly and offered me some of her orange to share but I did not feel like talking and continued to let the tears flow as the bus made its way back to the border.

Later in the trip, a Peruvian man, accompanying half a dozen tourists, started up a conversation with me across the aisle. I asked if there were any significant places to visit around Puno before I headed to Cusco where I would begin my journey home. He told me of a significant site that is not on the usual tourist route, called Amaru Muru, named after an ancient warrior who carried serpent wisdom. The place is known as a 'stargate'—a doorway or place where other dimensions can be accessed.

This is enough to get my interest, so I ask for clear directions to the site that is an hour by taxi from Puno. The English woman, Michelle, heard my conversation and was also interested in making the trip the next day. Before long we were exchanging stories of sacred sites and healing experiences around the world, and then we agreed to share a room together. In the evening Amber and I enjoyed a final parting dinner—this time with plenty of currency to enjoy a delicious meal of beautifully prepared local trout, followed by a dessert of local purple corn pudding. Then it was time for another emotional good-bye, as we reassured each other that she will be home in Australia in just one month's time.

I love the way chance meetings can send me in a completely new and stimulating direction when traveling, and this was no exception, as going to Amaru Muru is truly a mind-blowing experience. Michelle and I left Puno in a bright and sunny day, yet by the time we arrived at the stargate, the wind was blowing a gale and we had to wear every piece of clothing we had with us to protect ourselves from the icy blast. The taxi dropped us off and agreed to return two hours later.

The natural rock formations are absolutely stunning. The spirits of the land are strong here and everywhere we turned, there was a new amazing sight; in one direction a group of rock guardians sat, like little Buddhas watching over us. In another, a huge llama appeared to be looking out from the rock platform. An enormous symbol of an eye cut into the rock sat high up above us, and a pregnant Pachamama (Mother Earth) figure was slowly making her way across the valley.

We found a place to meditate, sitting on a rock shaped like an angel's wing, with some shelter from the wind. I am transported back to the Isla de la Luna and the Quechua spirit guide who offered me the conch shell from the lake, and my intuition guides me to symbolically bury the shell here at Amaru Muru. This creates a bridge of light between these two potent power centres, reaching from the land to the faraway island in the lake.

> *I sink down into the earth and Pachamama appears in front of me. She takes the shell and embraces me, hugging me tightly to her breast. I feel safe and held. She beckons me to follow her farther into the depths of the earth. We journey slowly down under Amaru Muru, as if walking an underground labyrinth into the womb of the earth. Our destination is a soft, dark timeless space, the void or place of unknowing, the great mystery. Pachamama tells me to sit and places the palm of her hand on my forehead, over my third eye. Intuitively I see the pattern of a labyrinth in her palm and understand the path of the feminine as a constantly*

> *moving cycle of life. Just as Mother Earth has her seasons and cycles, the times of inner exploration and healing must be in balance with the outward or social times, as must our acts of giving and receiving. I rest in the safety of the womb of the earth, feeling peaceful and grounded as this wisdom flows through my body.*

Later we crossed to the other side of the site, where the doorway, or stargate portal, sits. According to Inca legend, Amaru Muru is associated with the Golden Solar Disc of the Incas, located in Cusco at Corancha - the Temple of the Sun. When the Spanish conquistadors arrived in Peru, the Solar disk was hidden in the Monastery of the Seven Rays. Legend says the disk was then hidden in Lake Titicaca. When the warrior, Amaru Muru, left this reality, he walked into an unknown mystical dimension through this doorway. The columns on either side of the doorway are energetic channels for the masculine energy's downward energy spiral (Heaven to Earth), and the feminine energy's upward spiral (Earth to Heaven).

The 'gateway' is carved into an enormous rock and feels very balanced with these male and female energies. One side of the doorway appears to have a natural gold colouring in the rock, and the other side is white or silver in colour, perhaps symbolic of the sun and moon. The space of the doorway is about my height and I stood inside it with my back to the rock, looking out across the landscape in direct alignment with Lake Titicaca. I closed my eyes and felt centred; my sacral and solar plexus chakras gently adjusting themselves and coming into perfect balance. In my heart chakra, the heaven and earth portals met with the feeling of alignment for walking the path of an earth healer. The divine time is now and we already have 'heaven on earth'.

Shamanic Meeting

It was time to make my way home, so Michelle and I boarded yet another bus to Cusco. This time we went for the cheapest seats and forgot to ask for the 'directo' service that takes five hours and ended up on the one that stops in every small village. The journey took nearly eight hours along winding roads. Salesmen with a huge variety of goods, ranging from wheels of fresh cheese to vials of ginseng for good health, constantly hopped on the bus trying to make a living. Thankfully we sat in the front seats on the top deck where we could enjoy the changing scenery.

Gazing at the clouds and daydreaming, I realised I had dropped into another realm when the face of an indigenous shaman appeared in front of me. He had the strong features of a native Peruvian man with dark eyes and hair with a distinctive white streak in the front. His face hovered in front of me for a time, and I was curious why he had appeared to me, thinking perhaps he was a new spirit guide. Even though I am clairvoyant, I do not often envision people I have never met in the physical realm.

Finally the bus arrived at Cusco and we were bombarded with touts offering places to stay. We go with the first and most persistent woman who offered us accommodation in a guest house in the colonial area of San Blas, a quieter area of Cusco, known as the artisans' quarter and nowadays a bit of a hipster hangout.

The room rate was good, and after a bit of haggling for a larger room, we set out to explore the quaint cobblestone streets and alleyways of San Blas. There are strong Inca influences in this part of the city, which is reached by climbing the ancient Inca road, Hathunrumiyoc (Quecha for 'great stone street') from the Plaza des Armas in the centre of town. Michelle was looking for the Spanish school where she would study in the coming weeks and I was happy to wander after all the sitting on the bus.

We came to the Plaza San Blas and sat in the sun by its water feature. There were many small craft shops around the plaza, but only one caught my eye. It had the word 'MAGIC' in large golden letters above the door, and a window display with dream-catchers and paintings. I pushed open the heavy door, and as I entered the shop, the owner appeared from the back. He was the shaman from my vision! I was taken aback and shocked to see him manifest so quickly in physical form.

The shop has quite different jewellery compared to all the other local artisan offerings. The pieces here are unique and have different crystals and stones embedded in them. We start a conversation with the shaman, who is named Alfredo. He shared some of his family history and told us his shop is only open for fifteen days each month, as he also has a clinic in the Amazon where his family lives. Michelle was interested in a fire opal necklace for her heart chakra, and Alfredo gives her a psychic reading on how it could assist her healing process.

I am not shopping, as my travel money is coming to an end and I still need to pay for transport to the airport and last minute expenses. Alfredo goes inside and brings out a new piece, a talisman with several different crystals, a fossil claw and a baby condor feather. He explains that condor feathers are becoming rare because so many visitors now want them for shamanic purposes, and that the baby feathers are the only ones the chicks shed naturally before growing their adult feathers. The talisman is skilfully made and contains several different metals offering protection and balance. He tells me if I take the talisman, I must be prepared to do ceremony with it each full moon for the next nine months.

The ceremony involves wearing the pendant before the full moon each month, then burying it in the earth on the night when the moon is at its fullest point. The next morning you put it on again and sit in shamanic meditation, for which Alfredo gives me the instructions. During the first eight months I can release any personal difficulties and on the ninth month, my full healing powers will be restored. I still did not have the funds to buy the talisman and Michelle needed to get money to make her purchase, so we left with a promise to return the next day.

As we walk home, Michelle suddenly offers to pay for the talisman for me. I am amazed at this generous offer after such a short time of knowing each other. She is keen to support me in this way, and I offer her a healing session as a thank you. The next morning we collect our precious purchases, thanking Alfredo, and promising to complete the accompanying rituals.

I return home to Australia feeling supported and uplifted by my experiences in Bolivia and Peru. The time spent together with Amber is a heart-warming memory and completing another planetary chakra journey is another step in the bigger picture of my vision for visiting the sacred sites. I am grateful to have the magical talisman to give me focus and intention for the coming months as I prepare to put our family home on the market and to lovingly hand over the guardianship of the land.

I have always felt the truth of the Native American saying, *"The earth does not belong to us, we belong to the earth."* I believe we are custodians of the land for the time we reside there. We cannot own the land, and I am eternally grateful for the time we spent, living near the base of Mount Chincogan, where we established a deep connection with this little pocket of paradise and loved the land, trees and the wildlife and it loved us back ten-fold.

Healing Inspiration from Lake Titicaca – Sacral Chakra

❖ **Connecting with the Womb of Mother Earth**
It is wonderful to do this meditation outside in nature, where you can relax or lie on the earth and feel supported by the connection.

Feel your breath flowing gently in and out; with each exhalation, imagine you are sinking deeper into the comforting arms of Mother Earth. Become aware of your surroundings, taking in the elements – earth, air, fire, water – and ask for their support in this process. If you wish, you may call in a spirit guide, totem animal or angelic presence to accompany you; or you can choose to connect with Mother Earth (Pachamama) in a new way by asking her to present herself in physical form and walk with you as you journey inward.

Now visualise yourself entering the earth. You can do this by simply sinking down into the ground, or enter through an imaginary doorway that appears to you. Once inside you find a tunnel-like path leading deeper into the womb of Mother Earth. When you arrive in the sacred Womb Temple, take some time to get comfortable, notice the texture, colour and feel of this sacred space. You may prefer to relax and absorb the healing energy of the earth, or you may wish to ask questions of your guide. A sample question could be, "How can I balance my energies of giving and receiving?" or "Show me how to nourish my sensual self more". The answers will come to you intuitively in the form of a feeling, a word, a symbol or a gift. Allow yourself to absorb the subtle energy of the answer as you rest in the womb of the Mother and nurture yourself. Take your time and stay for as long as you wish.

❖ **Releasing Emotions for Healing**
As we clear our energy bodies and develop more sensitivity, we are far more likely to feel the effects of planetary changes on our emotions. The tides of the ocean are governed by the rotation of the moon and our bodies are made up of around

60% water, so it is not surprising for us to experience mood shifts and changes at different times. Women especially feel the changes of the moon cycles and subtle energetic currents of particular astrological influences, such as eclipses. We can also experience the emotions of other people close to us who may need healing, or situations of natural disaster can leave us feeling distressed and helpless.

We are all healers, and sometimes our natural healing abilities can go into over-drive wanting to support others. It can be difficult to identify what is your own energy and what belongs to another. When you find yourself experiencing unusual emotions or pain, you may have energetically corresponded with another person or an environmental situation and unconsciously tried to heal this by taking on the negative energy.

The emotional layer of the energy body is generated from the sacral chakra (Svadhistana) and calming your emotions by grounding this centre is a positive place to start. Visualise a gentle waterfall flowing from your second chakra. Imagine that any energy that is not your own is easily released through your grounding or roots. Any feelings that you are ready to let go of will automatically flow into the earth, where it is transformed into neutral energy by Mother Earth. As you cleanse your light body, you create the space for your own healing energy to support your ability to go with the flow and not against the current.

❖ *Honouring the Sacred Waters*

The indigenous shamans regularly hold ceremonies to bless and give thanks for the life-giving and healing properties of water. The Water Protectors of Standing Rock created the motto 'Water Is Life' and held the vision for clean water for all peoples and for future generations. Members of 300 tribes gathered peacefully in 2016, as a unified presence in support of preventing the building of an oil pipeline underneath a lake of the dammed up Missouri River on their tribal lands.

Water is receptive to our thoughts and feelings. This was demonstrated by the work of Japanese researcher, Dr.

Masaru Emoto, who believed that water was a 'blueprint for our reality' and that emotional energies and vibrations could change the physical structure of water. Emoto's water crystal experiments consisted of exposing water in glasses to different words, pictures or music, and then freezing and examining the crystal formations. This showed that water exposed to positive speech and thoughts would result in visually *pleasing* crystals being formed, and that negative intention would yield *ugly* frozen crystal formations. Emoto's book *The Hidden Messages in Water* was a *New York Times* best seller. [8]

Take the time to say a prayer of gratitude to the sacred waters of the earth. A simple "Thank you" to the healing properties of water in your local area can flow out through the streams, rivers and oceans around the world.

The ancient Hawaiian practice of Ho'oponopono for reconciliation and forgiveness is a beautiful blessing to offer to the water –

"I am sorry" – *"Please forgive me"* – *"Thank You"* – *"I love you"*

Lake Titicaca, Bolivia & Peru – Historical Facts

Lake Titicaca is the world's highest navigable lake at 3,856 metres (12,725 feet) above sea level. The lake borders Peru and Bolivia, with a surface area over 8,000 square kilometres. On the Bolivian part of the lake are two islands Isla del Sol and Isla de la Luna (Islands of the Sun and Moon). In 2000, an archaeological expedition discovered an enormous ancient temple submerged in the depths of lake, estimated to be between 1,000 and 1,500 years old. The Bolivian government has pledged funds to further study the ruins, however, locals are fearful about the effects that such disrespect of the sacred lake might bring. Perhaps the secrets of the lake are destined to stay beneath the calm surface.

Chapter 7

Base Chakra

Mount Shasta, California, North America

The Call of Native American Lands

In my imagination…

I am sitting on the slopes of a beautiful snow-covered mountain. My heart feels at home. The air is fresh and clear and I breathe deeply, filling my lungs with the negative ions and feel rejuvenated. A native spirit guide appears and invites me to follow him, leading me to a doorway in the side of the mountain. We enter through the opening into a dimly lit tunnel. I am not afraid, just curious. There is a warm glow coming from the end of the passage; my guide leads me towards this light. When we come closer I see the tunnel opens into a larger chamber filled with light from a golden flame in the centre. It is the Temple of Soul Contracts. I feel my vibration gently rising as I step into the temple. The healing has begun. My guide waits at the door and I take my time to settle into the expansive space, enjoying the cleansing and purifying properties of the flame.

After a time, a loving Being of Light steps forward to welcome me. This is the guardian of my soul contracts, who I may ask for guidance or assistance with their completion. I choose to focus on a difficult relationship. The Light Being produces a scroll relating to this soul contract and tells me I must forgive both the other, and myself, in order to set myself free from the ties of this past-time agreement. Visualising the person standing in front of me, I complete a 'surrender, forgive and release' ritual, repeating this three times, to set us both free. Finally I feel the scroll with the karmic agreement completely dissolve into the flame. At the same time, an aspect of myself that did not feel recognised in the relationship returns to me in a gentle process of soul retrieval.

My aura is now radiating with golden light and the energy of unconditional love permeates my whole being. I may return to this sanctuary for healing and support whenever I wish. For now I feel complete as I thank the guardian and return through the tunnel with my guide to emerge into a sparkling nature land.

Nature Orgasm

North America was not high on my list of places to visit. I had been to California in my early twenties, and whilst we had lots of fun, I did not feel a strong connection to the land at the time. It was many years later when I visited Sedona in Arizona, known for its natural vortexes, or swirling centres of high energy, that I had a profound experience with nature. Although it is not one of the primary earth chakras, Sedona is a powerful sacred site in its own right and a place where I hoped to explore the strong resonance I felt with Native American teachings.

As the calling became louder, a friend told me about a healer who had created a unique range of flower essences living near Bellingen, New South Wales. Her name was Kaliana Rose and through a series of synchronistic events, I found myself on my way to meet her. My children were still small and we were on a holiday with their grandparents, so leaving them in capable hands, I squeezed in a brief time-out at the beach to ground and centre myself before our meeting. As I closed my eyes to meditate, my Native American spirit guide, Chief Adario, appeared. In previous shamanic journeys, he had given me a feathered cloak to wear as protection, and also in recognition of my soul connection with Native American teachings.

I felt Chief Adario standing in front of me as the feathers of my ceremonial cloak fluttered in the breeze. I saw his familiar face, with deep-coloured skin and wrinkles of laughter and wisdom. He looked directly into my eyes and said "You must give Kaliana the cloak". I was shocked, and a feeling of ownership of the cloak arose. Fears started to reveal themselves of no longer being worthy of wearing the cloak. Yet I also felt his request was right and true.

In my visualisation, I untied the cloak and gently pulled it around into my arms, ready to pass it on. Then an amazing thing happened; I felt a blanket of new baby-sized feathers begin to shoot from my back. Within minutes a new cloak of rainbow-coloured feathers had formed. I let my tears flow as I recognised my fear of lack and felt the message arise of 'sharing from the heart creates more abundance'.

As soon as Kaliana opened the door, we felt a sisterhood bond. I initially felt shy to share that I had a 'gift' for her that was non-physical and came from my spirit guide! At the time I was not used to sharing spiritual messages with strangers, and this was a big step in trusting my intuitive guidance. However, I had nothing to fear; Kaliana received the cloak gracefully and felt it was to support her grieving process following the death of her father. We spent some time talking about our healing work and our visions.

Kaliana had been to Sedona, and as we said good-bye, she unexpectedly gifted me a beautiful pair of Native American porcupine quill earrings with the words "May these earrings take you there." I put them on and wore them often in the coming months.

Later that year my husband and I made the difficult decision to separate. On the last Christmas we spent together, he surprised me with the gift of an air ticket to Sedona. I was nervous about travelling alone, but knew I needed clarity about my next step as a single mother, and how to navigate the challenges of co-parenting. Taking time away on a vision quest was the perfect way to reconnect with myself and begin my healing process.

I scoured the pages of *Lonely Planet* and found a holistic retreat centre, complete with geodesic domes, in the forest surrounded by the red rock mountains. It offered a sauna, steam room, spa and meditation dome – this all sounded perfect to support my time away.

It was mid-January and chilly when I arrived in Phoenix. After a good night's sleep at an airport hotel, I collected a rental car and set off on Interstate 17. The freeway was clear and I enjoyed being alone on the open road. Within two hours I was taking my exit and the magnificent red rocks of Sedona rose in front of me. Their colour and shape reminded me of Kata-tjuta (The Olgas), the iconic rock formations in the Red Centre of Uluru National Park, back home in Australia.

I received a warm welcome at the retreat centre and was immediately invited to join a small group of residents and visitors for a full moon drumming circle at Cathedral Rock. It had been snowing, so I dressed warmly, thankful for the borrowed down jacket to keep me cosy, and we set off into the clear moonlit night.

Sedona has four major vortexes surrounding the small town; Cathedral Rock is one of these centres. A vortex is a vibrational field that creates a funnel shape of spiralling energy – just as water creates a spiral when going down a drain. The heightened energy resonates from the centre of the vortex in a radius of around half a kilometre. There are further potent power spots to be found along the trails and in the amazing gorges of Arizona, including the magnificent Grand Canyon.

We climb up to one of the lower platforms at Cathedral Rock and gather together in a circle. One of the locals has an enormous mother drum, large enough for a group of people to play together. There are others with medicine drums and a didgeridoo being played by a German visitor. There is magic in the air and I immediately feel the intense vibration of the vortex. When the drumming begins, I drift into a trance-like state. I lie back on the rock to take in the extraordinary view of the towering rocks and the luminous moon lighting up the crystal clear sky. High above me a plane creates a contrail as it crosses in front of the moon, and beneath me the resonance of the drumbeat vibrates through the rock. My breathing slows to the familiar rhythm. My healing has begun.

Over the next few days, I explored several of the trails and opened to the transformative energy of the vortexes. I make friends with one of the residents at the healing centre, a beautiful man named Bo, who is a recovered alcoholic. He has completed a twelve-step programme and has a spiritual practice to support his recovery. I have a familiar sense of recognition with Bo, as if we already know each other from another lifetime and we are immediately comfortable in each other's company. We take a couple of fun day trips together and it is on one of these excursions that an astonishing thing happens.

I have become used to driving on the opposite side of the road and can now take in the spectacular scenery as I drive. Bo dozes off in the passenger seat beside me as we head towards one of the vortexes recognised for its property of balancing masculine and feminine energy. I turn a corner and the magnificent Bell Rock is right there in front of me. I catch my breath and feel the landscape begin to merge with me. My heart chakra opens to receive the beauty of the land and suddenly I am overcome with ecstasy, as an orgasm of the heart vibrates throughout my being.

The experience leaves me breathless. I have never felt such a deep, intense and unexpected connection with nature before. I find a safe place to pull off the road to integrate this profound encounter. I can only guess that the powerful energies here have heightened the sensitivity of my own chakras and translated my increased awareness of nature into bliss. Naturally, Bo is disappointed that he missed out on witnessing this ecstatic moment!

On another occasion, we go for a walk in Oak Creek Canyon to visit a place known as the Fairy Pools. In the middle of the creek there is Mushroom Rock where people choose to get married in this tranquil setting. Bo and I walk through a field and along the creek bank to find this private spot. At the water's edge, he sits respectfully on the bank while I climb onto the large flat rock to meditate. The sound of the water finding its course around the rocks is soothing and calming.

I create a spontaneous nature ritual, giving thanks to the water as I visualise it flowing through my aura and cleansing my chakras, preparing me for my new unmarried life back in Australia. I allow myself to cry tears of release and drink in the replenishing properties of the water. Finally, I turn my face to the sun to feel its nurturing warmth and reach my hands to the sky in gratitude for the many gifts of healing I have received here.

I am totally absorbed in my ceremony and it is only when I look up to step across the creek that I see Bo gazing at me with so much love. "The beauty of woman in sacred ceremony", he says, "I am privileged to witness your celebration". I feel touched by these words, from a man I barely know, and I send out a silent prayer to invite a man with respect and honouring for the feminine into my life.

Rocking my Foundations

My initial calling to journey to all the places indicated on the earth chakra map had begun in 1988 when I made the intention to travel to the power centres. Twenty-eight years later, in 2016, I had almost finished my quest to visit all of the major earth chakras. The only site I had not been to was Mount Shasta in Northern California. My business partner had been there, and for some time I thought a personal pilgrimage to this sacred mountain was not necessary.

The earth chakra essences were my 'baby', mostly created when I was traveling alone, except for a couple of occasions when friends had been with me, such as in Egypt and the group trip to Uluru. However, in 2010 my business partner offered to visit Mount Shasta to make the base chakra essence, as she would be spending time in California. This made sense, as I had no idea when I could get there myself. I followed this in 2012 with my trip to Lake Titicaca for the sacral chakra so the range of seven Sacred Planet Essences was complete, or so I thought.

What occurred next was a complete shock to me. Later I would see it as an experience of enormous learning and growth, but at the time it rocked my foundation. After eighteen years of working together, my business partner unexpectedly made the decision to end our collaboration. This decision in itself was not a problem for me, I was more than happy for us to go our separate ways and focus on our individual projects. But I was left feeling devastated by the ending of, not only the business relationship, but also the withdrawal from our long-term friendship. I could not see an opening for resolution and felt immobilised by the situation. The deep pain I experienced felt like a dagger in my heart. The intensity of my feelings would only later become clear to me.

As well as grieving the loss of a dear friend, the parting shattered my illusion of creating a secure base in partnership with another, and pushed me into an intense time of soul searching. I rediscovered a truth that I thought I already knew, "I can create security and safety for myself – no-one else can do this for me". I realised the business partnership had begun immediately after my marriage ended, when I was still in the healing process. I now understood that when I rely on someone else, even in subtle ways to support me, it does not allow me to anchor my own secure grounding and let myself shine. When I do sit fully grounded and present in my base chakra, I can choose to collaborate with others, without losing my own connection to a stable foundation.

I also became aware of slipping into an old co-dependent pattern of holding high expectations of others and then feeling disappointed when my anticipations are not met. When I caught myself falling back into old negative ways of relating, I made the choice to practice forgiveness. This helped me to let go of my attachment to a resolution, focusing instead on the understanding that no-one is to blame and allowing me to see that both parties are doing the best they possibly can in any given situation.

The enormous grief and loss took many months to heal, and required much self-exploration and inner reflection. I recognised the karmic link that joined us had made it difficult for me to let go, yet part of me also understood the relationship was no longer serving our souls in working together. In time, I came to a place of love, forgiveness and compassion. I feel enormous gratitude for our friendship, including the loving support, immense spiritual growth and all the laughter along the way.

During this time of healing, Kaliana Rose offered me a session that gave me greater insight to finally resolve the situation within myself. And I finally gained the clarity I was seeking.

Sisterhood Healing

I am inside a sacred cave with a group of women in Southern France. I feel the soft darkness of the temple and the awareness that each one of us carries the essence of the Sacred Feminine. I see myself grounded in my feminine 'birthing doula' self, with the violet flame of transformation glowing softly in the centre of the circle. The flame is a symbol of the wisdom and teachings of the Sacred Feminine that was hidden for safekeeping during times of patriarchy. Sadly, all is not well in the Sisterhood, there is conflict between the women and some of them believe they are the sole custodians of the flame. The flame cannot be owned; in truth the eternal flame is free to all.

Suddenly the feeling of wishing to die floods over me and I see myself surrendering to being stabbed in my solar plexus, pointing towards my heart. I have decided to surrender to death and leave my body rather than confront the conflict between my sisters. In death, my spirit splits off from my physical body—the aspect of myself that implicitly trusts in spirit and in the sacred feminine is now floating far above me. I clearly see the separation within myself and the way it has been reflected back to me by others. I am guided to reconnect with this part and I call my soul back to integrate the aspects of earth and spirit in my heart. I can now stand fully empowered in the secure foundation of my sacred feminine.

To support the healing, Kaliana gave me a vibrational essence called *Sovereignty* – for remembrance of True Self and Purpose. The remedy is to help with taking self-responsibility, letting go of being a victim through honouring of the self and the choices made in life, by realising and claiming the soul learning.

I am enormously grateful for the close circle of supportive friends, women and men, who 'midwifed' me through this difficult time of rebirth, transformation and stepping into my power in a new way. When I reflected on the enormous lessons I had learnt relating to my foundation, I realised it was essential for me to visit Mount Shasta, the planetary base chakra, myself. I am not sure how I could have thought any differently. My pilgrimage to the earth chakras was a significant mission on my soul path and a vision I had been holding for 28 years. It was now obvious to me that I must personally stand on each one of these power centres around the world to complete my quest. And visiting Mount Shasta was pivotal in supporting me to connect with a solid base in my own personal power.

Magic Mountain

In astrological terms, there is a particular planetary phenomenon called the Saturn Return, which occurs about every 28 years of a person's life. This event is a time of coming into alignment with your life's true path. The planet Saturn will give very clear signals if you are not aligned with your calling and pursuing your passions. For me, at age 28, this signal was a serious skiing accident in which I dislocated my right hip. Lying flat on my back, with my leg in traction, forced me to take time out to review my life and make the final decision to leave my successful career in England and follow my dreams to Australia.

There is a second Saturn Return that happens between 56 and 60 years of age. This can be another challenging period when big changes in work, relationships and other areas of life occur. During this time we may revisit familiar themes, but hopefully we now have the experience, wisdom and greater clarity about what we want to accomplish in life. Many people retire around their second Saturn Return, when they finally feel the freedom to explore new ideas or interests that have been on the back burner for some time. This event also marks an initiation into the role of an elder or wise woman, and taking on a position as mentor or guide to younger generations.

Ultimately, the energy of Saturn pushes us to take responsibility and face our limiting core beliefs. These two cycles of the Saturn Return bring any areas where we feel restricted, limited, deprived or fearful to the surface for us to confront. The question "Who is the author of my life?" can be asked in order to reclaim our own authority for lasting success and inner satisfaction. Perhaps it was not just coincidence that I was right in the throes of my second Saturn Return during the dissolution of the business partnership.

When I emerged from the grieving process, it became absolutely clear that I must write my story as a personal memoir, and that I now had the time and freedom to focus on this creative project. I began to write, hesitantly at first, and then with surprising focus, as the words flowed through me. I wrote mostly from memory, apart from referring to the many journals that I kept on my travels that helped me recall specific details. I was keen to finish the book before my 60th birthday, but first I needed to get to Mount Shasta.

In 2016, my daughter Amber was living in Madrid doing a university exchange, and I planned to visit her in the European summer. I managed to find a round-the-world ticket that allowed me to stop in San Francisco on the way to Spain. Friends, Jack and Yvonne, in nearby Marin County, generously invited me to stay with them. I was very busy in the lead up to my trip, and had no time to anticipate how my time with the sacred mountain would unfold. As always, I trusted the guidance would come when I arrived there.

I took the shuttle bus from the airport to Marin, crossing over the Bay on the iconic Golden Gate Bridge. Next to Sydney, I feel San

Francisco is one of the most beautiful cities in the world, and in fact the two places have many similarities in lifestyle. I enjoyed a relaxing week, taking in the expansive views of the water from Yvonne's deck and getting to know the local area.

I have timed my trip to Mount Shasta to coincide with the full moon weekend in May known as the Wesak Festival, or Buddha's birthday. This is an auspicious time in the Buddhist spiritual calendar, when it is believed greater expansion of consciousness is possible than at other times of the year. At the time of Wesak, two streams of energy, one from the Buddha and the other from the Christ, are blended to unite East and West in a shared holy day.

The name Wesak comes from a legendary ceremony held in a Himalayan valley when the Buddha is said to bless an assembled gathering of Enlightened Beings – from the Christ to the most humble disciple. At the exact time of the full moon, the participants meditate in silence to hold the inner connection for this potent blessing. All around the world, spiritual groups gather to align with the essence of enlightenment in the Wesak valley and to take time out from daily life. I was excited to join a gathering at Mount Shasta.

The road is clear for the five-hour drive to Mount Shasta, and as I get closer, the scenery changes to the dense fir and pine trees of the Siskiyou National Forest. The scenic route cuts through the mountains and crosses a bridge high over the blue waters of Shasta Lake. I am headed for McCloud, a small village just outside Shasta City, where I have booked accommodation at the Timber Inn. The quaint lodge is run by a local guy in his mid-fifties who tells me he has never ventured far away from the mountain he calls home. When he hears I am from Australia, we have a friendly chat about the amazing places he has seen on the National Geographic Channel and in his dreams, but he says is unlikely to ever leave home.

I settle into my room and then drive into Mt. Shasta. I have my first glimpse of the enchanted mountain. Mount Shasta or White Mountain (Úytaahkoo in the language of the Karuk Tribe) is covered in snow for many months of the year. In May, the crêpe myrtle trees are flowering and their vibrant pink blossoms contrast brightly against the vivid blue sky and the pure white snow on the mountain. The town has a laid-back feel with wide streets and very little traffic. This suits me as I am still remembering how to drive on the other side of the road. I have to pay attention at each of the crossroads to follow the American rule of allowing the first vehicle to the intersection right-of-way, regardless of which direction they are turning. This is quite different to Australia where those going straight ahead have priority.

Mount Shasta has become a centre for spiritual seekers and those wishing to retreat in the clear air and beauty of the mountains. There are many New Age outlets, yoga centres, crystal shops and every kind of healer, psychic reader, angel intuitive, meditation coach and shamanic practitioner you can imagine. It is very much like my Australian home-town, Byron Bay, and I feel quite at home. Earth chakras and significant places of power naturally attract those on a spiritual path. The uplifting energy supports our own transformation and growth, making it easier to share our healing gifts with others.

Another positive aspect to the influx of visitors is a thriving health food store with an organic café and huge range of takeaway products. I enjoy a delicious vegetarian dinner with an almond milk chai, before stocking up for breakfast and my trip up the mountain the next morning. The waitress tells me to "watch out for deer" on my drive home, a good reminder for me to stay alert, but I do not meet a soul on the road through the forest and happily snuggle into bed to dream of the magic mountain.

Mount Shasta is sacred to the Native American people and Hopi legends talk about a vast network of caves and an underground city. In more recent times, spiritual seekers have viewed it as a place where connections with spirit guides, angels, spaceships and UFOs are regular events. There are reports of the Ascended Masters, spiritually advanced beings who assist human evolution and radiate the luminous essence of divine love, being seen on the slopes of Mount Shasta, including St. Germain, known as the Master of the Violet Flame. In 1987, during the *Harmonic Convergence,* one of the world's first globally synchronised meditation events, Mount Shasta was named as one of a small number of global power centres.

A collective belief is that the mountain is home to a hidden city from the lost continent of Lemuria (also known as Mu)—an ancient civilisation that once covered a vast area, including part of the United States, Canada and extended to Hawaii, New Zealand and Fiji. This etheric city is called Telos. It is a higher vibrational place and also known as 'The Crystal City of Light of the Seven Rays'. Those who have contact with the Telosians describe them as beautiful, tall (over 7 feet) fifth dimensional beings, who are both ageless and timeless. It is said their gift to us is one of awakening and raising our vibration to the loving level of the heart.

I believe the Lemurian existence was one of non-duality and non-separation, living with an absence of power and control issues. Instead, the inhabitants related harmoniously, with balanced male/female energies and an easy flow of loving communication. During readings with people who have a Lemurian lineage, I see a strong connection with the element of water – the ocean, the mer-people, the shell kingdom – and they are most at home near the beach or a large body of water. I, myself, have a sweet past-life recall of Lemuria – living as a *mermaid* in an underwater temple in the spiral shape of a nautilus shell. My soul sister, Janie, shares the same memory and we remember it as a blissful and playful time together.

There is no doubt that the mountain has a mystical power and exudes the energy of peace and harmony. It sits like a guardian watching over the whole region. The aura of Mount Shasta is pyramid shaped, pointing to the heavens, with another inverted pyramid of light reaching deep into the core of Mother Earth. This six-pointed star acts as a conduit or entry point for the light-grids of the planet.

In sacred geometry, the merkaba (3-dimensional six-pointed star), is symbolic of merging the divine with the physical realm, bringing feminine and masculine energies into perfect equilibrium, while offering spiritual transformation. Mer means the connecting thread - light, Ka means the spirit or astral self and Ba means the body or physical self. This potent symbol represents 'Heaven on Earth', the infinite potential to live a life of bliss here on earth—*As Above, So Below.*

In one of the spiritual shops, I find a beautiful card with an image of the mountain and these words –

> **Prayer to the Sacred Mountain**
> *(author unknown)*
>
> *Mount Shasta*
> *Is often called the 'Tibet' of the Western world,*
> *To Her, the Light of Heaven has Come...*

In Activation of the 7th, and last Sacred Mountain,
Now She Calls
As the Font of Knowledge an of Truth
To the Earth and To All of Humanity...
Come...
The Call has Gone Forth...
And You are Welcomed

The next morning I go to collect pure water from the headwaters of the Sacramento River, which emerge in the Mount Shasta City Park. This mountain glacier water travels through stone and sediment before reaching ground level and many people come here to drink from the crystalline spring and enjoy its healing properties. Those living nearby believe in the magic the water offers to body and spirit, and bring large containers to fill for everyday refreshment.

Feeling energised by the water, I set off up the mountain. The sun is shining and the road is cleared of snow so I have little appreciation of the conditions at higher altitude. I have read about Panther Meadows many years ago, and a picture of the many wildflowers growing high on the mountain enchanted me, so this is where I am headed. I reach the cleared parking area and set off to find the flower-filled meadows. Walking along the path, I feel excited by the crispness of the air, it has a purity to it and I realise this is the only essence to be created in snow.

Before long, I am trudging through deep snow, without a wild flower in sight, and it becomes obvious I am here long before the meadows are in full bloom. I look around and ask for guidance on the right location for the essence. I notice a large rock to the side of the path and as I get closer I see it is heart-shaped. It is the perfect spot.

I immediately feel the presence of a Native American Elder spirit guide. He is checking me out as I sit to meditate, and then welcomes me to his sacred lands. As always, I offer a prayer to the ancestors and guardians of the land and ask for permission to be here before setting up the essence. There is a sense of spring in the air and I gather fresh green ferns with soft moss to support the bowl of pure water. The only people I see during my time here are two snowmobile riders calling out joyfully as they fly down the snowy track.

I feel completely held by the magic of the mountain and the stillness of the freshly fallen snow. The bright sunshine warms my face and the sweet pine smell of the Douglas firs fills the air. Through the trees I see the forest spreading across the nearby mountain range, as far as my gaze can see, to the vivid blue horizon. The mother tincture captures the essence of this stunning landscape and offers support for a secure and tranquil foundation in the base chakra.

There is an atmosphere of deep peace as I reflect on this culmination of my twenty-eight-year pilgrimage to the sacred sites. I am centred and grounded in my connection to Mother Earth. I know this is my true foundation and the only nourishment I need to satisfy my life purpose. I now rest in quiet fulfilment.

Wesak Festival

A gathering of like-hearted souls come together each year to celebrate Wesak in Mount Shasta, held at a lodge in the park where the spring waters of the Sacramento River emerge. At this powerful time of the Scorpio full moon, an eclectic group of speakers offer presentations on all things spiritual, from intuitive healing and support for the highly sensitive, to crystal skull teachings and shamanic journeys. For me this was an opportunity to hear stories of transformation from the enchanted City of Telos and to connect with local mystics and healers.

The presentation on *Highly Sensitive People* catches my interest, as I work with so many clients who are sensitive and take on other people's pain. Many of them feel ungrounded and disconnected from spirit or source. Trying to avoid 'negative' energy only compounds the feelings of isolation and can lead to depression. Often people with depression do not sit comfortably in their own base chakra and find it difficult to stay connected with the earth.

For those who are highly sensitive, accepting you are an *empath* is the first step towards making positive changes in daily life. Learning to fine-tune your intuitive gifts, perhaps with the help of a teacher, to differentiate between your own energy that of another, and to regularly clear your aura and chakras is essential to stay grounded. From this secure place it is possible to *hold space* for others without holding onto their pain. In England, where I grew up, the term *sensitive* is often used to describe a person who is clairvoyant, psychic or a medium, I have even had friends tell me "You talk to the spirits, you're a sensitive" and I take this as a compliment.

One of the presenters at the gathering was Raymond Tarpey, a Mayan historian and the caretaker of a beautiful blue agate crystal skull, named EarthKeeper. His presentation on the *Crystal Skulls and the Spiritual Legacies of Mu/Lemuria & Atlantis* was enlightening and I enjoyed talking with him about visiting the ancient temples in Mexico, one of my next planned adventures. 9

The Mayan legend of the 13 Crystal Skulls speaks of a time when all the skulls will come together to support a transformational shift in consciousness for humanity. Presently 12 of the skulls have been found in different places around the planet, primarily in the Equatorial regions. The most famous of these is the Mitchell-Hedges skull, allegedly discovered in 1924 by Anna Mitchell-Hedges in a disused temple in Belize, although scientists question this story.

The spiritual belief about the original crystal skulls is they are pre-Atlantean, created together by 13 Masters who shaped them through the highest sonic vibration and then carried them to various locations. They are carriers of ancient wisdom, imbued with special powers and profound healing abilities. My own experience of meeting EarthKeeper, and of meditating with other crystal skulls, has been a heart-opening state of unconditional love, peace and balance. The time of the crystal skulls reuniting may well be close, as we collectively continue to raise our consciousness and hold the collective vision for peace on earth.

This legend of wisdom-keepers coming together also correlates with the more recent convening of the 13 Indigenous Grandmothers who held their first gathering in 2005 in New Mexico, USA. The Grandmothers were brought together by a common vision of unity and have created an alliance of prayer, education and healing for Mother Earth, for all her inhabitants, all the children and for the next seven generations to come. They have held 13 gatherings to date and I had the pleasure of meeting two of the Grandmothers a few years ago when they visited Byron Bay. I was inspired by their grounded presence, deep wisdom and unconditional love for the earth and for us all.

As the Wesak Festival comes to a close, a local presenter, Ashalyn, who is an author and healer, guides us through a meditation to visit the golden City of Telos deep within Mount Shasta.

Again I am greeted by the Native American spirit guide who invites me to enter through a golden archway. Once inside, a female guide welcomes me and together we appear to float through deep walls of gold light until we come to a central chamber that is a healing temple. I feel the gentle presence of Saint Germain, and see the violet flame glowing brightly in the centre. The violet flame carries the qualities of purification, forgiveness and compassion. I am invited to ask for healing for any aspects of my life where I am not living my highest destiny. I request support to integrate and complete my earth chakra pilgrimage and the writing of my book. I surrender the negative beliefs that may hold me back—lack of self-confidence, unworthiness, fear of being judged or criticised. These thought-forms are purified by the violet flame as I release them into the light.

As I focus on forgiveness of myself and others, I feel my heart chakra opening with compassion. I visualise a smaller violet flame in the centre of my base chakra supporting me to create a new foundation of living in my truth with clarity and loving compassion. The flame expands throughout my chakras, physical body and aura–raising my vibration to match the healing energy of the violet ray. I become aware of my soul family surrounding me and pouring unconditional love into my heart chakra, connecting us all together as one. Taking the time to breathe in my experience, I gently emerge from the healing temple with renewed confidence to continue on my path.

Later, browsing the exhibitor stands, I enjoy chatting with a local publisher. When I mention my book about the earth chakras, she responds enthusiastically, she then asks: "Where are you placing Mount Shasta?" adding quickly, "Many people believe it represents the base chakra, but we see the mountain as the eighth chakra, sitting just above the crown!" I smile to myself, trusting that I have come full circle and that this, too, is the truth.

This final chakra journey has strengthened my own foundation and connection to life. I feel deep gratitude for this blessing and for the profound healing inspiration I have received from the earth chakras all over the world.

Healing Inspiration from Mount Shasta – Base Chakra

❖ *Grounding into Mother Earth*

As a spiritual being having a physical experience, you are able to drift in and out of your body. This happens at night and in your dreams and also when we travel around the planet to different countries. At other times if you are in shock, frightened or simply uncomfortable being here on the earth plane, it may be easier to leave your body. Creating a supportive connection with Mother Earth is a simple and powerful way to release stress and anchor yourself back here in present time.

Give yourself about ten minutes of uninterrupted time for this meditation, the practice is best done first thing in the morning or during the day when you are not feeling tired. Ideally, sit in on a cushion on the ground or in a comfortable straight-backed chair with feet flat on the floor, let your hands rest with palms up on your thighs and with softly closed eyes.

Find your natural breathing pattern, take several deep breaths and tune into yourself. How are you feeling? How is your physical body? Are you distracted by anything that's running through your mind? Have the intention to release any concerns/tension/pain/tightness from your physical body with the outward breath.

Focus your attention on welcoming your spirit back into your energy field. Imagine you are calling your spirit back from any places or people where you may have left your energy behind. Invite yourself in fully. As you connect with your spirit you will feel more centred and secure in your body. Staying grounded allows you to handle day to day stress more easily.

Now become aware of your Aura: the subtle energy field that is inter-connected with the chakras and extends out in layers beyond your physical body. Feel yourself sitting in your own auric field, which is egg shaped and reaches about a metre all the way around you.

As you sit comfortably in your body, focus on your base

chakra (Mooladhara) Tune into the chakra and notice how it feels – are you aware of it spinning? How open or closed is it? Does it have a colour? Just observe this, as you ask your base chakra to come into 'present time', this may slow in down a little or perhaps help it to flow more easily.

Next bring your focus to Mother Earth – check in with her today, she is constantly evolving and changing. Ask her to show you the best possible place to ground into – you may see a literal place, or sense the energy, that feels most comfortable for you today.

Allow a hollow 'grounding cord' to form, from your base chakra. Send this grounding deeply down into the centre of Mother Earth. Anchor the cord into the earth, then check to see how connected you feel. Have the intention that your grounding cord will be set on gentle release and anything that you are ready to let go of will automatically flow into the Earth, where it is transformed into neutral energy by Mother Earth.

Breathe into your base chakra, your foundation, the qualities of security, balance and greater flexibility in present time. Sit quietly for a few minutes, breathing gently and allowing a feeling of peace and calm to fill your body. To complete the cycle, visualise soft sunlight pouring in through your crown chakra and filling you with golden light, allow this to flow into each chakra and continue on down into Mother Earth as a blessing of gratitude.

When you are ready open your eyes. During the day check-in to see if you feel more present in your body. Make an intention to practice the meditation each day this week, becoming aware of any changes and making a note of them in your journal.

❖ Connecting with your Tribe

The base chakra relates not only to our present time foundation, but also to our ancestors and our cultural heritage. Our family of origin does not always support or accept the unique choices we make in life, particularly if we step out of the paradigm of being seen as 'normal'.

Following your soul path will guide you in a new, and often alternative, direction. Finding your tribe will offer you the support and acceptance to be yourself. For women, join a women's circle, where you can safely express yourself and feel nurtured in all the stages of womanhood. For men, join a men's group or activity that empowers you in your masculinity and creates supportive bonds

We are becoming a global family and many of us are called to travel around the world, to expand our awareness in different cultures, and perhaps to live in places far away from the place of our birth. For some this may mean having two (or more) places you now call *home*. Wherever your home is at any one time, make the intention to connect with your tribe, those people who you feel an inner knowing with and a soul resonance that is beyond biological imprint. Being surrounded by your soul family supports the expression of your true self and strengthens your divine connection in a more grounded way here on earth.

❖ Walking Gently on the Earth

Native American teachings share the concept of walking the *Beauty Way*. The principle of *natural order* when we are aligned with the cardinal directions (East, North, West and South), the cycles of the seasons and respect for nature. There are so many ways we can give back to Mother Earth. Caring for the earth must come from our heart in the way in which we feel personally called to serve. This could be something simple such as tending to our small garden, growing vegetables or picking up rubbish on our morning walk. It need not be traveling to far-away places, although if this is your calling I am the first one to encourage following this call!

When we walk gently on the earth there is no past or future—only present time in which we can draw on cellular memory to access our own healing. Remember you are an expansive multi-dimensional being. All of your soul's vast experience exists within you now. If you do feel called to a particular place on the planet, endeavour to go there, it undoubtedly carries soul growth and healing for you. Trust your intuition, when you experience inner-knowing or gut feelings and follow your inner guidance system. Collecting pictures of the place or sacred site is the perfect way to begin aligning with the ancient teachings and energies to which you are being drawn. Whichever way you choose to respect the earth make it your devotional practice or 'seva' (selfless service), something that makes your heart sing and connects you with the Mother Earth in a grounded and heartfelt way.

Mount Shasta, North America – Historical Facts

Mount Shasta in Northern California is a dormant volcano and not part of any mountain range. With a summit of 14,125 feet above sea level, her often snow-covered slopes rise abruptly nearly 10,000 feet above the surrounding landscape. Shasta is a popular destination for spiritual travellers, mystics, gurus and sages. The mountain is said to have a strong connection to the ancient civilisation of Lemuria and there are endless unexplained stories of visions and healing experiences that have taken place here.

Giving Birth and Beyond

Writing a book is like giving birth, it is an inner process, calling on the author to connect with their own deep resource of trust and belief. The conception of the idea slowly becomes a blooming pregnancy, as the words begin to emerge and pour onto the page. The long months of nurturing and nourishing the outline pass by, with many hours of sitting and waiting for inspiration. When it is finally the time to birth the baby, the waves of expansion (contractions) begin gently at first, allowing the writer to embrace the flow of labour and to find a rhythm, to focus, to breathe and to let go of fears.

The labour moves along beautifully, until it comes closer to birthing, when the more intense stage of transition hits, usually just prior to the movement of the baby down the birth canal. This is when the mother feels most open and vulnerable. The birthing hormones are at their peak and feeling safe and supported is vital. Fears may arise, such as "I can't do this", "I want to go home" or even "I want a caesarean!"

For the author, questions of self-doubt such as "Whatever gave me the idea to write a book?" or "No one will want to read my book anyway", may compromise the next stage. Drawing on the inner resources of trust and connection to the 'spirits of writing', plus a loving support team, the birth will be accomplished and the baby welcomed into the world. Finally to complete the process comes the placenta, the amazing organ that has been the lifeline between mother and child in the womb, and this will be my next pilgrimage.

For many years I have been fascinated by the teachings of an Aboriginal Elder, Minmia, Wirradjirri Law Woman and Teacher. She talks of the importance of belonging to *Country* and the indigenous belief that we belong to the oneness of Creation and the great significance of the place of our birth. The ritual of burying the placenta in the earth where we are born anchors us to the teachings of the land and activates our life destiny and purpose. If this does not happen, the growing child may feel like a lost soul.

In her book, *Under the Quandong Tree,* Minmia shares *"If you are born of this land, you are of this land, and therefore you are entitled to the teaching of this land by birth. And for those not born of this land, they can belong by doing the Rebirth Ceremony."* [10]

I have now lived in Australia for exactly half my life, the same number of years that I lived in England. This is where I belong, and is the place I call home. It is time for my own Rebirth Ceremony, to anchor my placenta and my soul blueprint more consciously into Australia. I plan to take my 'baby', this book, back to the sacred rock, the place where I was first called by the spirits of the land, and where my path took a fresh and unexpected direction.

Looking back on the many twists, turns and transformations I have experienced in following my soul calling over the past 28 years, it is difficult to imagine how my life may have evolved had I continued to live in England. During this time, I have let go of doubts, such as *"Am I on my Soul Path?"* and learnt to see each life event as cumulative to my soul purpose. It is often in looking back that we truly understand the significance of individual moments as key learning experiences in life.

Like many women, becoming a mother has been the most transformative event in my life. Giving birth to my two daughters has given me the power to trust my intuition and believe in myself, a gift that has supported and guided me over and over on my travels. My daughters are now both seasoned travellers, and I trust they too will continue to follow their hearts whenever the calling arises.

I know travel is part of my destiny, with my moon sign in Sagittarius, one of the greatest travellers of all the zodiacal signs. Traveling is one way to accelerate my spiritual growth. This may explain my ongoing desire to get on-board a plane at any opportunity and the feeling of having my wings clipped whenever I am not able to venture very far. I believe my soul intention this lifetime is one of gathering many different experiences and learning through those cultures and events.

Each one of the earth chakras I have visited, and the numerous detours, has been significant on my healing journey. The people I have met along the way have all been part of the intricate thread that weaves our soul connection together. I now have a deep well of wisdom to drink from whenever I feel uncertain or fearful. The blessings from the sacred sites continue to inspire and support me as I take the next step on my soul path.

From my home in Byron Bay, the most easterly point in Australia, and place of the first light, I align myself in the present moment gently opening my heart to be guided into my future. A golden bridge of light connects me with each of the earth chakras. I am grounded in my sovereignty and held in the embrace of our sacred earth. I embody the healing I have received from the earth's chakras and in deep gratitude share this wisdom.

Crown Chakra – Machu Picchu
I breathe in the rejuvenating power and abundance from the radiant sun.

Third Eye Chakra – Varanasi
I hold a vision for peace on earth as I meditate upon the holy waters.

Throat Chakra – Great Pyramid –
I appreciate the power of words and the sacredness of silence.

Heart Chakra – Glastonbury
I open my heart to the healing power of the earth through nature.

Solar Plexus Chakra – Uluru
I sit in stillness with respect for the Indigenous elders and earth-keepers.

Sacral Chakra – Lake Titicaca
I connect with the womb of Mother Earth to receive emotional healing.

Base Chakra – Mount Shasta
I ground deeply into the earth and my secure foundation in life.

Acknowledgements

With heartfelt thanks and gratitude to all of my teachers, soul family and friends who have supported me, not only in the writing of this book but in walking beside me on my life path. Your trust and belief in me inspires me to shine my light brighter.

My women's circle, your ever-present holding through the labour, transition and waiting for the next wave to birth myself anew is doula-ing at its finest.

Special thanks to those who physically supported the birth of Sacred Earth Wisdom. My editor, Azriel Re'Shel, your encouragement, word skills and our shared knowledge of the sacred sites has made the editing process a pleasurable one. To Jack Travis, you gave me the masculine perspective, positive feedback, editing expertise and plenty of laughs too.

For my daughters, Jade Aditya and Amber Selena, becoming a parent is by far the greatest journey I have ever taken. Thank you for choosing me as your mother, for the gift of our soul connection and for being an on-going source of strength and inspiration to me by simply being your beautiful selves.

I am blessed to walk on the earth at this time when the opportunity to travel far and wide is a safe and easy one. I am eternally grateful for the wisdom of the sacred sites; they have given me soul growth beyond measure. My deepest gratitude is to Gaia – Mother Earth herself.

About the Author

Anna Watts is a pilgrim, spiritual healer, sacred birth educator and mother.

Over the past 28 years she has worked with thousands of clients supporting and mentoring them through soul growth and transformation. She is passionate about the chakras and works intensively with these psychic energy centres or 'wheels of light' that hold the keys to spiritual awakening.

Her pilgrimage to the earth's chakras, and meeting with spiritual teachers around the world, has greatly enhanced her understanding of the magical, the mystical, the shamanic and the way indigenous cultures embrace healing as part of daily life.

Anna is an inspiring speaker and teacher, she offers **Spirit Way** workshops in spiritual development, chakra balancing and healing, supporting others to use their intuitive gifts and healing abilities.

The founder of **Celebration of Birth,** Anna educates parents, Doulas (birth attendants) and Pre-natal Yoga Teachers in the art of sacred birthing, and also runs women's circles.

She is co-author of the **'Birthing the Spirit'** cards and guidebook, providing inspirational guidance for Conception, Pregnancy, Birth and Babymoon. Anna sees sacred birthing as pivotal to world peace: *"As we birth our babies more consciously, we plant the seeds of wholeness for future generations".*

Anna calls Australia home and lives in the lush hinterland of Byron Bay, Northern New South Wales.

Spirit Way offers insights and guidance for holistic wellbeing and connection to Mother Earth. Supporting balance and spiritual growth; healing of the mind/body/spirit to raise your vibration and embrace life more fully.

- **Sacred Planet Essences**
- **Spiritual Healing Retreats**
- **Sacred Tours to Sacred Sites**
- **Training in Spiritual Healing**
- **Spiritual Healing Sessions**
- **Chakra Balancing Readings**

Healing sessions and readings are available anywhere in the world via Skype.

To find out more about how Spirit Way can support your spiritual journey visit –

www.spiritwayhealing.com.au

Facebook – Spirit Way Healing with Anna Watts

Instagram - #sacredbirthsacredearth

References

1. Paulo Coelho, *The Pilgrimage* Harper Collins USA (1995)
2. Robert Coon, *Earth Chakras* Robert Coon (2009)
3. Drunvalo Melchizedek, Serpent of Light Beyond 2012: the Movement of the Earth's Kundalini and the Rise of Female Light Weiser Books (2008)
4. Drunvalo Melchizedek, Serpent of Light Beyond 2012: the Movement of the Earth's Kundalini and the Rise of Female Light Weiser Books (2008)
5. Anna Watts, *Creating Chakra Altars*, www.spiritwayhealing.com.au /courses/chakra-journey
6. Uncle Bob Randall, *Kanyini* Hopscotch Films (2006), www.kanyini.org
7. HRH Dalai Lama, *Ten Eternal Questions: Wisdom, Insight, and Reflection for Life's Journey* by Zoe Sallis Chronicle Books (2006)
8. Dr Masaru Emoto, www.masaru-emoto.net/english/water-crystal
9. Raymond Tarpey, www.raymondtarpey.com
10. Minmia, www.minmia.com.au/site/

www.ingramcontent.com/pod-product-compliance
Lightning Source LLC
Chambersburg PA
CBHW031419290426
44110CB00011B/443